Accelerating Business and IT Change:
Transforming Project Delivery

To our wives

Accelerating Business and IT Change:
Transforming Project Delivery

ALAN FOWLER AND DENNIS LOCK

GOWER

Published by
Gower Publishing Limited
Gower House
Croft Road
Aldershot
Hampshire GU11 3HR
England

Gower Publishing Company
Suite 420
101 Cherry Street
Burlington,
VT 05401-4405
USA

British Library Cataloguing in Publication Data
 Fowler, Alan
  Accelerating business and IT change : transforming project
  delivery
  1.Project management 2.Information technology - Management
  I.Title II.Lock, Dennis
  658.4'04

  ISBN-10: 0 566 08604 2

Library of Congress Cataloging-in-Publication Data
Fowler, Alan.
  Accelerating business and IT change : transforming project delivery / by Alan Fowler and Dennis Lock.
     p. cm.
  Includes bibliographical references and index.
  ISBN 0-566-08604-2
  1. Project management. 2. Information technology--Management. I. Lock, Dennis. II. Title.

  HD69.P75F69 2006
  658.4'06--dc22

                                                                  2006002754

Printed and bound in Great Britain by MPG Books Ltd. Bodmin, Cornwall

Contents

List of Figures

Preface

One thing above all has characterized the general perception of business change and IT projects to the present day, and that is their proneness to failure. A high proportion of projects are delivered late, grossly overspent or even flawed in performance. This book explains some of the common reasons for such failures. More importantly, we recommend radically new methods developed by Isochron that have been proven over a number of years and in a variety of clients to be highly effective in delivering the project outcomes that stakeholders expect.

People who have become frustrated through apparently inevitable project delivery slippages and budget excesses should find this book refreshing. Isochron takes a novel approach to how established project management practices can be retained and used within a framework of new thinking, methodology and portfolio management. Nothing here contradicts the current good practices encapsulated in PRINCE 2 and well-established project management techniques (such as those promoted by the Association for Project Management and the Project Management Institute). This is a marriage of ideas, old and very new, that together represent an exciting quantum change in delivering projects on time, within budget and to the satisfaction of investors.

Finance and project portfolio managers will find that the techniques explained in this book provide them with the means to drill down, track and (if necessary) challenge the cash values of project *benefits* as well as the costs. For example, one finance director reported, on seeing reported results from a project managed by these methods, 'For the first time I have been given a mechanism that allows me to get a handle on the black hole that is IT expenditure.'

Project sponsors need a practical way in which to express their expectations and requirements. In particular, they need an alternative to numerical measures to express their needs for procedural and behavioural change in a recognizable, routine way. This book shows how they can improve the certainty with which they can get the results they want.

Businesspeople and project managers understand that finishing the IT element of a project is only a step or two along the road to final success. They know that no project is successfully finished until it has delivered its return on investment. These same people also know the importance of the end customer, and they appreciate that ways have to be found to create and control change in communities of stakeholders. Whilst there are instructive precedents for mass change of beliefs and behaviours in communities (and even whole countries) the science of how to do this in businesses is new. Techniques for such change thread through this text, using methods that can create and control change in communities of stakeholders.

Our ideas were developed with 'soft-target' projects of business and IT change in mind, in contrast to projects that produce buildings, plant, bridges and other environmental outcomes. To our surprise we have since had feedback from people involved in engineering and construction projects which indicates that they, too, find the Isochron techniques described here to be valuable. We hope that you will find them valuable too.

Alan Fowler
Edinburgh, 2006

Acknowledgments

This book was conceived in June 2003 at Henley Management College, where the early members of Isochron – Richard Scott, Tony Carter, David Franks, Andrew Holmes, Bernie Hopkins, Derick James and Cindy Morelli, joined by Greg Hawes – met with me in an attempt to write a 50 000-word book in two days. The final compilation has taken a little longer, principally owing to work pressures on the original team members. In 2005 Gower introduced Dennis Lock to the scene. Dennis rewrote the book with me, using a mixture of old-world courtesy, humour and gentle goading. I owe the completion of this work to him.

Experienced project managers will find ideas in this book that are old friends and much that is plain commonsense, but they will also discover much that is new to management literature – ideas that are unique and crucial to the impact of our recommended methods for project success. The pioneering insights for these innovations have come in large measure from clients' observations and from far-reaching discussions and arguments in offices, hotel lobbies, on walks and beside fires with David Franks and Duncan Davidson.

For the original research and academic guidance we owe much to Ken Currie, then a memeber of the Artificial Intelligence Applications Institute in Edinburgh and to Phil McKell and Graham Smith, then members of the Turing Institute in Glasgow. We are also indebted to Professor Henk Sol and his colleague Alexander Verbraek, who gave us the environment, context and encouragement to present and publish the early research at the International Conferences on Dynamic Modelling of Information Systems hosted by Delft Technical University in the 1980s and 1990s.

The techniques described in this book would not have emerged without the extensive practical experiences provided by John Blakeley's company in Hamilton, UK; by Herb Jacobson and his company, particularly by Jack Durner in Boston, US; and by John Duncanson and his Glasgow team. To the best of our knowledge, it was Hal Sullivan of Ernst & Young who first used the term 'value flashpoint' in a sense close to that now used by Isochron and as described in our text.

I acknowledge the significance of the commercial approach adopted by Alex Mackie, then of Scottish Hydro Electric, in managing their transformation programme in the 1990s. I also pay tribute to Clive Williams of Ernst & Young, who instructed me to carry out the Ernst & Young UK transformation programme of 1997 in five months with no budget and 'none of that programme management nonsense'. Also in connection with that Ernst & Young programme I acknowledge

Mark Molyneux, who gave me all the authority and backing for which a programme manager could wish. Without the extraordinary challenge at Ernst & Young we would never have invented recognition events and backcast planning.

Colin Winchester and Martin Brown, when at Martin Currie Investment Management, gave us a unique early opportunity to roll out some of our new approaches in a comprehensive set in one company and we are indebted to Pat Cox for following that project through to full commercial impact in what would now be called SIM – Service Infrastructure Implementation. Sean Sullivan of United Utilities gave us the chance to repeat the business case and some of the benefit realization techniques in many different contexts.

New developments are, of course, built upon the shoulders of giants. The giants we acknowledge are those thousands of heroic project managers whose IT and business projects have been perceived to have failed and who have suffered personal stress, disappointment and blame as a result. We salute them and acknowledge the debt of learning that we owe them. The memetics of memes (ideas) are as complex and vast as the genetics of genes. I acknowledge gratefully all of these people and the scores of others whom we could list if space allowed.

Alan Fowler

About the Authors

ALAN FOWLER

In the course of his career Alan has been involved in most aspects of business and has coupled this with unique experience in business change and in the administration, management and building of major IT systems, both as a user and as a provider. He has extensive experience in change management, programming, systems analysis, project management, structured methods, procurement, quality, and teaching.

Alan's first encounter with computing and projects was in 1973 in the Central Computer and Telecommunications Agency, where he was part of a team purchasing IT for Government departments. In the CCTA he had training in mercantile law and gained experience of contracts and procurement which he has found valuable throughout his subsequent career. In due course Alan transferred to the then Scottish Office (now the Scottish Executive), where he gained in-depth experience of management of finance and a detailed grounding in computing, structured analysis and in operational, project and personnel management.

In 1985 the new emphasis on enterprise under the reforms of the Thatcher government provoked Alan to move out of the public sector into a small consulting, software and training firm engaged with large corporate clients. He gained a practical appreciation of the realities of all aspects of managing and running business. In a large finance company he encountered the difficulty people have in comprehending and managing concurrent streams of work, and through this became interested in development of designs for business exhibiting rapid change characteristics. With the help of colleagues, in 1989 and 1991 Alan published research papers on this subject at the International Working Conferences on Dynamic Information Systems based at Delft Technical University.

In 1991 Alan joined Ernst & Young's Management Consulting Services and played a significant role in the successful growth of their Scottish business. He worked in three major programmes in clients and was involved in several pieces of due diligence work, experiences that enabled him to apply his research privately and develop his ideas for accelerating change. When Ernst & Young (E&Y) made consulting into a national function, Alan facilitated the reorganization of E&Y UK and then went on to manage the business continuity preparations for the year 2000. As this work approached completion he moved back into client-facing work with Ernst & Young's Government Services group, working in connection with major modernization programmes in the Department of Work and Pensions and the Inland Revenue. Throughout this time Alan privately used the results of his own practical applications of the research carried out in 1988–1991.

In 2000 Alan left Ernst & Young to become a founder director of a healthcare eprocurement company and at the same time to provide selective private independent consulting in accelerating programmes and projects. At the end of 2002 he re-incorporated his own private business as Isochron Ltd., a UK-wide membership company specializing in a range of innovative techniques for the acceleration of projects and complex programmes, outcome-based project management and realisation of project benefits. Alan took the results of his practical applications of his research and assembled and branded them for Isochron. In 2002 he was invited to prepare a new project management regime for Martin Currie Investment Management, which gave an early opportunity to deploy many of the techniques in a coherent set and to see the impact of them across a company's performance thereafter.

Isochron provides a stimulating and challenging membership network and service for authoritative senior people with more than 20 years' experience in business and more than 10 years in the field of programme and project management. Through some of its members and associates it is able to provide a teaching, consulting and delivery service to its clients to apply the Isochron techniques in their programmes, projects and business, whilst carrying on researching and developing new practical techniques for project management. Its ambitious objective is to transform project delivery by 2010 as much as lean engineering transformed car manufacturing in the 1970s.

Alan is a Fellow of the Royal Society of Arts, Commerce and Manufactures. He has lectured at the QA Forum, the IBM Annual Conference, BPPM and at numerous other meetings, and has been a regular lecturer for the Institute of Chartered Accountants of Scotland. He is a past member of the Institute's IT Committee.

DENNIS LOCK

Dennis Lock began his career in the laboratories of the General Electric Company, mainly designing and prototyping electronics equipment for defence. Through part time study he obtained a Higher National Certificate in applied physics. His 15 years with the GEC were interrupted twice, once by conscripted service with the Royal Air Force and again by three years as a project engineer with Ardente Acoustics, in the very different but morally rewarding industry of subminiature hearing aids. Five enjoyable years followed as a manager with various divisions of Honeywell Controls and it was at the end of that employment, in 1968, that Gower published his first book, *Project Management*. His book was instantly successful, partly through its clear writing style (which Dennis has always strived to achieve) and not least because it was the first British book to treat project management holistically, rather than as simply a number of scheduling and other techniques.

From 1968 to 1971 Dennis was Manager, Engineering Administrative Services with Herbert-Ingersoll, which introduced Dennis to the world of heavy engineering, giant machine tools and some savage examples of management politics. He has long been indebted to the directors of Herbert-Ingersoll for allowing him free reign to develop very successful project management methods that, even today, are still considered advanced. These techniques were specially directed towards multiproject cost and resource scheduling, using critical path methods, with emphasis on the efficiency that is available to most (but adopted and understood by few) using modular networks and templates.

In 1971 Dennis joined the international mining company Selection Trust, and held a succession of management posts with them until 1987, during which time the company underwent several management and ownership changes, eventually becoming Seltrust Engineering, a company within the Minerals division of British Petroleum (this division is now part of Rio Tinto). He was finally responsible for many head office activities of Seltrust Engineering, including purchasing, project management procedures, estates management, reprographics and facilities management.

Since 1968 Dennis has undertaken a number of consultancy assignments, both for his employers and independently, in the UK, the US and in Europe. In 1994 he was invited to join the masters programme of an English university, lecturing to MSc and MBA students on courses that included project management as a subject and later, in 2000, he doubled this activity by joining the external staff of another highly regarded university.

Dennis Lock continued his writing activities without interruption since the publication of his first book and has written or edited over 30 titles (mostly for Gower) plus countless contributions to other books and professional journals. He is now a full-time freelance writer, specializing in project management and related subjects.

Dennis is a Fellow of the Association for Project Management, Fellow of the Institute of Management Services and a Member of the Chartered Management Institute. In the past he and his wife have kept exotic pets and indulged in mountain walking, but now he spends most of his time staring into his computer, working on his next publication.

CHAPTER **1** *Recognizing Project Success*

Most people would agree that the principal purpose of project management is to achieve a successful outcome for the project. This introductory chapter starts by considering factors for determining project success and explains why every project manager should have a clear vision of the project in its finished, successful state.

INTRODUCTION

This book can best be introduced by telling some stories. All good nursery stories begin 'Once upon a time' and most point a moral. Our stories are no exception but, unlike most nursery tales, they are matters of fact:

- Once upon a time we built cars the 'fat' way. *Nowadays* we use lean engineering, working backwards from the customer's needs. We get rid of all the procedures that don't add value.
- Once upon a time we built ships one at a time, one after the other. *Nowadays* we build ships two or three at a time, in parallel and in tandem, collaborating simultaneous component development from around the world.
- Once upon a time we built houses from the bottom up, brick by brick. *Nowadays* we assemble preconstructed modules into the building structures; 'delivering higher quality homes in one-third of the time and at lower cost' (quoted from promotional literature).
- Once upon a time we carried out IT and business change projects step by painful step, moving slowly forwards from the project start. *Nowadays* sadly, we still do.

This story has as yet no happy ending: nothing much has changed. Of course methods have improved, but no fundamentally new approach has been developed to match modern progress in the building of cars, ships and houses. We have made no equivalent dramatic breakthrough in project management.

PROJECT MANAGEMENT: FOR FAILURE OR SUCCESS?

If the purpose of project management is to achieve successful outcomes for projects, we should expect all the effort to be focused on those outcomes. But it seldom is. Most of us will usually discuss in detail the processes and activities that are happening in and around our projects. Ask us to discuss the risks and problems and we will mention the external suppliers, job deadlines, overruns and shortfalls against the work schedules and plans for today, tomorrow and next month. Ask us about the overall outcomes of our projects and we will give the briefest of statements, often implying that project success is in some way dependent on other people and organizations.

The skills and tasks of a project manager are about the processes and jobs of running a project. The picture presented by many projects is of an army of ants, swarming over myriad tasks, happy to be mentally challenged and busily employed, with all thoughts of an end postponed. The end of the project is seen as a close of the participants' present employment. Attention is focused on the next task or deliverable item. 'Sufficient unto the day are the problems thereof' (Matthew 6:34). It all seems a million miles from emulating the breakthroughs to higher efficiency achieved in car manufacture by Toyota in the 1970s, Korean shipbuilding in the 1980s and by the worldwide construction industry in the 1990s.

This focus on day-to-day, week-to-week and month-to-month working instead of the final outcome, sets up enormous tensions between the project team, the project sponsor and those investing in the project. Those who pay the piper expect to call the tune, but project progress reports too often highlight the viewpoints of the project manager and team – not the issues and progress related to the outcome of the project. Progress reports classically describe the technical problems, the immediate needs for resources and decisions of the project team and workers. The report language is often so technical as to be meaningless to the sponsor and investors.

Once an outcome is lost to the sight of those working in the project there is a high probability that their efforts will diverge from the minimum necessary path. They will find themselves discovering details and problems that had not been foreseen. In losing sight of the final outcome, no one will notice which details and problems are irrelevant. Work will expand to fill (and overflow) the time and resources available.

In projects where there is a way to describe the outcome in clear and tangible terms, it is possible to communicate that outcome in terms that the entire team can understand. The team can then visualize the objective, focus their collective effort and avoid wasteful diversions. This is relatively easy to achieve in engineering and construction projects. In the military context also, every member of the battle team is utterly clear about the objective. The 'project management' of a battle provides excellent lessons about making the objectives tangible and communicating them consistently to every person involved.

This book is about the enabling methods that lead to a revolution towards the outcome-based management of IT and business change projects. Just like the car manufacturers we will use lean engineering. We shall emulate the shipbuilders by collaborating simultaneous component development. Like the modern construction companies, we will assemble preconstructed modules into our project structures.

How can all this be achieved simply? Our answers are based on the discoveries, experience and successes of Isochron. That company's thinking has revolutionized the efficiency of projects, with the result that they can be accelerated towards meeting the goals of their sponsoring organizations.

OBJECTIVES AND FACTORS FOR SUCCESS IN DIFFERENT KINDS OF PROJECT

The way by which project success is measured – indeed, the ideal way by which a project is managed – depends to some extent on the nature of the project. Lock (2003) has identified four main project categories. This classification, although somewhat simplistic, is useful in the context of considering project management procedures and objectives and is illustrated in Figure 1.1.

We should start by dismissing the last category of projects identified in Figure 1.1 (Category 4) as being irrelevant to our discussion. Category 4 includes only projects carried out for pure scientific research, where attempts are made to advance

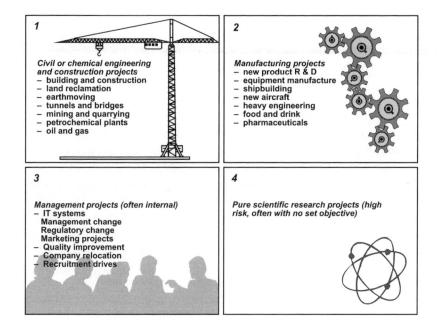

Figure 1.1   Four project categories

the frontiers of knowledge. When the research is purely experimental, it may not be possible to set any objectives at all, and the benefits can range from nil to unexpected heights. Traditional project management methods cannot be applied because there is usually no time plan and the work does not lend itself easily to scheduling. It is possible to limit risks and exercise some management control by stage-gating, which means having periodic reviews, each of which is linked to the release of fresh funds or a decision to end the research. But Category 4 projects are outside the scope of this book and will not be mentioned again.

Projects in Categories 1 and 2 have been the main focus of specialist project management practice, publications and training for well over half a century. Their management methods have many similarities. The principal differences are that projects in Category 1 (civil engineering, construction and so forth) are usually conducted in the open air, away from the main contractor's home office and are to a large extent visible to the public, whereas manufacturing projects (Category 2) take place in walled or fenced environments on the main contractor's premises and out of the public gaze. All these projects have tangible outcomes. When they are finished, there is obvious physical evidence of construction or a manufactured product. The principal indicators of success or failure can be expressed in terms of technical and commercial performance, all easily quantifiable in numerical units of measurement (including monetary units). Another feature of these projects is that most of them are carried out by one organization for another, usually within the strictures of a commercial contract. When the project has been finished and handed over, the main contractor or manufacturer moves on to something new, leaving the project owner to operate and maintain the physical outcome of the project. Of course, many projects have lasting commercial and environmental results but, so far as the project manager and contractor are concerned, the principal benefits should all be realized when the project work is finished and the user makes the final payment and takes over responsibility for operation and maintenance (shown in Figure 1.2).

Category 3 includes business, IT and change management change projects, which are carried out internally. Although external suppliers, contractors and consultants might be needed, it is the internal project owner who is ultimately responsible for managing the project and implementing its changes. All funding for these projects comes from within the company. There is often no tangible outcome, only a change in the business processes, technology, roles, procedures, behaviours, attitudes and beliefs. The intention is to improve the business in some way that creates value. Initially, project costs will considerably exceed the value of the intended benefits. Most of these benefits will not be realized until near or after the end of the project. They may comprise one, two or all of the following:

• an immediate cut in costs (such as when staff leave the payroll)
• an immediate cash receipt (for example, when payment is received for a new product or for the sale of assets rendered redundant by the project)

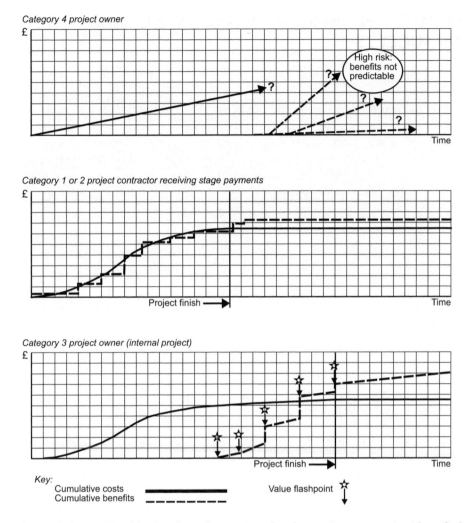

Figure 1.2   Possible cost–benefit patterns for the project categories identified in Figure 1.1

- continued improvement in cash inflows resulting from the project (either as cost savings or increased revenue)
- an increase in the assets and intangible value of the company.

The Isochron approach described throughout this book identifies each occasion on which one of these cash benefits is expected as a 'value flashpoint'. This concept will be explained at greater length in due course (particularly in Chapter 3) but it is introduced and illustrated in Figure 1.2. In brief, value flashpoints are predictable and easily recognizable events that are directly associated with cash savings or benefits that should result from the project.

IMPOSED NUMERICAL TARGETS: NO GUARANTEE OF SUCCESS

The imposition of numerical targets is a popular and traditional method for attempting to improve performance, in people, in projects and in business activities generally. Further, if precise targets can be set at the beginning, why should these not eventually provide the benchmark for deciding whether or not the project has ended with a successful outcome? Target-setting is seen at all levels in a business, from the lowest departments up to senior management and beyond, and indeed gave rise some years ago to the 'management by objectives' process. Used sensibly, and with discretion, target-setting has considerable merit. But setting numerical objectives alone is no guarantee of success and can run the risk of producing negative results.

Consider the following scenario. Salespeople are given new goals to meet, production managers are asked to improve productivity by x or y per cent, or a materials manager could be told to cut the inventory turn rate. All these objectives are defined precisely in terms of numbers or percentages. This performance-measuring method has been greatly favoured by the UK government, which sets targets to reduce waiting times for National Health Service patients, for class sizes in schools, for crime figures in the police forces and so on.

At first sight, setting numerical targets seems laudable; it seems to offer a sure-fire path to success by motivating people to improve their work performance and meet specific, qualified performance targets. But what usually happens in practice? Experience proves that those who have targets imposed upon them are often motivated in ways different from those envisaged by their superiors. Danger comes from regarding the targets themselves as the sole motivators, regardless of their effects on the people subjected to them. Organizations and people are placed under unreasoned pressure to 'get the numbers right'. So, for example, salespeople can become tempted to fudge the figures in their reports or, worse, sell at unprofitable prices to achieve their targets. In one extreme manufacturing example, an operative was set a quota of products to deliver each day from the end of his production line. He exceeded his daily quota simply by removing products from the end of the production line and feeding them back on to the conveyor belt upstream!

In 2005 the UK government set general practitioners a target of seeing every patient within two days of making an appointment. According to complaints from the public to the media, some doctors simply stopped making appointments for more than two days ahead, thus achieving their target at a stroke. The result of this insistence on a numerical target was that many patients found great difficulty in making appointments because, once the current two days of their doctor's diary had been filled, callers were asked to try again the following day and, if necessary, the day after that and so on until an appointment slot became available. Frustrated patients were forced to make repeated calls to overloaded switchboards before they could finally get their appointment.

Members of a team of immigration administrators were given permission to leave work early each day, provided they had finished a set quota of received application cards. One administrator achieved high numbers, enabling her to leave her desk and go home early on most days. Years later, the building was demolished. A small hole in the wall of the ladies' cloakroom gave access to the lift shaft, at the foot of which the demolition workers found thousands of incomplete cards.

It is evident from these and many other examples that the imposition of numerical targets on people and organizations is no guarantee of achieving true success or business improvement. We need, therefore, to take a fresh look at intended project benefits and the paths by which they can be achieved and recognized.

FROM IDEA TO BENEFIT HINDSIGHT

Isochron methodology views the aims and benefits of new projects from a different perspective from that taken by the conventional numerical target-setters. It does not immediately ask the question 'What targets should we set for this project?' but instead takes a more farsighted view, an imaginative look into the future. It realizes that the attainment of numerical objectives depends on changes to behaviour, beliefs, roles, procedures and processes. It seeks to visualize differences in the ways in which the business and its staff will be operating when the desired level of improved business performance has been achieved. What will be the behavioural indicators in people and the organization that will signal true success?

Of course there are underlying target aspirations, but these must not be allowed to become the drivers. Get the human and systems behaviour right, and the targeted numerical results will follow. This is a notion that is not always easily grasped and it runs counter to tradition. But the method and its advantages will become clearer through the following examples.

Office accommodation example

Suppose that a building society has decided to merge with another and close the two old, outdated headquarters offices and build one new corporate headquarters. New IT systems and office procedures will be implemented as part of the move so that the commercial systems of the two previously separate companies are fully integrated. The target-setters might set new preferred staffing levels and define accommodation requirements and standards as so many square metres per staff of each grade, listing other amenities and then getting the building designed strictly on the basis of the numbers to be housed and the space needed for equipment, and so on.

Using a more imaginative approach, the change sponsor and senior management must envisage how they want the new offices to look and feel when they are built and occupied, and consider the kind of working environment they wish to create for the staff. They have to ask *and answer* many questions, along the lines of the following examples:

- What new behaviours would they like to see happening?
- If an individual in the new office were asked to describe the objectives of his job, what would they like him or her to say?
- What new procedures do they expect to see and which old procedures will have ceased?
- What new roles do they expect to see people filling and which old roles will have disappeared?
- What new types of meeting do they expect to find and, when they inspect them, who will be attending and what will the agenda be?
- Which old types of meeting will have been discontinued?
- What new technology do they expect to see being used? What old technology will have disappeared?

In addition, the change sponsor and senior management will have to foresee the experiences and perceptions of clients who telephone or visit the new office.

So far, there is nothing about setting numerical targets to improve personal or overall business performance. However, tangible cash benefits will result, and these can be prophesied and imagined as future value flashpoints. Here are some examples:

- Removal from the old office means so that maintenance costs are immediately reduced, noticeable by the closure of various building maintenance contracts.
- Proceeds from subsequent sale of the old office are received into the accounts.
- Termination of the lease on the old office has been negotiated successfully. This was previously payable at £500 000 on each quarter day. (The first quarter day on which the payment no longer falls due is a value flashpoint.)
- Identification and removal of duplicated jobs from the previous two companies has allowed the release of 20 staff. (The day on which the costs of those 20 no longer appear in the payroll is a value flashpoint.)

Remember that the above list does not report historical events, but forecasts future events that can be imagined by the sponsor and senior management when they consider the outcome of the successful project. Isochron calls these *recognition events*.

A business restructuring case

Megacover plc is a large insurance company with its main offices in the City of London. The group has decided that it needs to re-examine its structure and organization. Currently it is organized by technical functions so that, among others, there is a finance group, a customer services department and a claims department. Each of these groups and departments handles a mix of motor, home, commercial and travel insurance. Consultants have advised, and the company has agreed, that the organization should be product based in place of the existing functional organization.

So, using the Isochron approach, the sponsor and senior management are asked to visualize the effects of the project as they change the behaviour, beliefs, roles, procedures and processes amongst the various members of staff in the organization. Suppose that a member of the current customer services department were to be asked today about his or her work. The answer might be: 'I work in the customer services department, surrounded by the customer services department team. We all work on the third floor and I report to the customer services department manager. We have monthly meetings to discuss workload and improvements.'

Now imagine asking the same person the same question when the reorganization is complete. The answer should now be: 'I work as a customer services agent within the motor team on the fifth floor. Around me sit the claims and finance staff who specialize and liaise with me in motor insurance. I report to the head of the motor insurance team. Every two weeks we have a meeting of customer services representatives, claims and finance to discuss our operational statistics and plan our activity. The operational statistics report is a new functionality within our IT system.'

'Where', you now ask, 'is the original customer services department manager?' The answer comes: 'We no longer need a customer services department and the manager was given early retirement.'

Remember that these dialogues have not yet taken place. They express the outcome of a project as required by senior management while it is still in its proposal stages.

'But', you might say, 'we know that measurement is a fundamental means of making change happen, and of getting our expectations met. What you measure is what you get. If you say that we should not set numerical targets, how can we make change happen?' There are two parts to the answer:

1. Changes in behaviour, beliefs, roles, procedures and processes can be described in terms of specific, dated events that can be inspected and recognized. These 'recognition events' are matters of fact. For each of them we declare the exact date, the place, the context and the person involved so that an appointment can be made in the future to inspect it. On their expected dates they either will or will not have happened. They are just as absolute, and have as much effect. as numerical targets.
2. The changes in behaviour, beliefs, roles, procedures and processes lead inevitably to the changes in numerical measures that we want. We should continue to set numerical targets which we expect to see achieved, but they will happen as a consequence of, and should not be set as the motivator of, changes in behaviour, beliefs, roles, procedures and processes.

CONCLUSION

Success in managing business change projects comes from creating a project climate that encourages people to adapt their work behaviour in ways that will inevitably lead to sustainable improvements in company performance. Achieve this, and the numerical results will follow automatically. By contrast, if you set numerical targets you will get behaviours that you didn't expect or want and, ultimately, numerical results that you also didn't want. Our approach, which has been demonstrated and proved in several radical IT and business change programmes can produce results as spectacular as those in the car, shipbuilding and construction industry stories that opened this chapter. It delivers higher quality, because it enables the whole project to be focused on the sponsor's and paymaster's expectations. It does so in less elapsed time because the associated techniques allow compression of the plan and minimization of interdependency. Costs and consumption of resources are reduced, because everyone in the project team is enabled to differentiate between what would be wasted effort and what is essential.

REFERENCES AND FURTHER READING

Buttrick, R. (2000), *Project Workout*, London: Pearson Education.

Fowler, A.K., Franks, D.J. and Currie, K. (1990), 'The Application of Parallelism in Commercial Dynamic Information Systems' in *Proceedings of the International Working Conference on Dynamic Modelling of Information Systems*, TUDelft.

Fowler, A.K., Franks, D.J. and Currie, K. (1992), 'The Dynamics of Commercial Processes: Concurrency of Events and Episodes' in *Proceedings of the Third International Working Conference on Dynamic Modelling of Information Systems*, TUDelft.

Lock, D. (2003), *Project Management*, 8th edn., Aldershot: Gower.

Womack, J.P., Jones, D. and Roos, D. (1990), *The Machine that Changed the World: The Story of Lean Production*, New York: Simon & Schuster.

2 *Benefits, Business Opportunities and Theats*

Business change and IT projects are always intended to enhance the business in some way, but the path to hell is paved with good intentions. This chapter discusses some of the preliminary factors to be considered when selecting a project (as a precursor to the preparation of a detailed business case as described in Chapter 3). The discussion is taken beyond consideration of a single project to building a portfolio of projects and deciding which projects in the portfolio should claim priority for action and expenditure of resources. The common theme (common in this chapter but unfortunately not so common in practice) is ensuring that the benefits of every project admitted to the portfolio align with corporate objectives.

PROJECTS AND THEIR ALIGNMENT WITH CORPORATE OBJECTIVES

It should be obvious that every new project and every portfolio of projects should contribute in some significant and measurable way to company objectives. However, the ideas for projects can originate in many different places, often among those who might have little or no awareness of the company's strategy and overall aims. Business change and IT projects, even when successful, can involve enormous expense and cause considerable disruption throughout the organization. The consequences of failure are potentially devastating; hindering or even stopping the organization's daily business and operations, damaging tangible and intangible assets, wrecking market reputation and causing distress or even despair among the staff (the most important asset of all).

Drucker (1967) looked at the question of how staff (and, in particular, senior executives) divided their time between work that was directed to achieving company objectives and work that was not. He suggested that every executive should frequently ask the self-examining question: 'How is what I am doing contributing to my company's objectives?' The same type of question should be applied to the selection of every new project: 'How will this project contribute to or align with the company's objectives?'

Later in this chapter we shall recommend how this question can be answered in terms of value drivers, which themselves are vital elements of the business case. Too many instances exist where this question has not been asked and answered effectively before committing valuable time and resources to projects.

The potential for success or failure

Jones (1996) pointed out that really large software systems can 'cost more than building a domed football stadium'. In the late 1990s, for example, one UK government department alone commissioned IT development and change projects during an 18-month period in the following sums (which together, accounted for a commitment of over half a billion pounds sterling):

- one project in the £50–60 million bracket
- one project in the £40–50 million bracket
- one project in the £30–40 million bracket
- one project in the £20–30 million bracket
- six projects in the £10–20 million bracket
- nineteen projects in the £1–10 million bracket.

Isochron's studies of a sample of eight IT developments and business change programmes carried out in private-sector companies in the UK through the period 1996–98 yielded the following total cost statistics:

International investment bank	£500 million
Utility company	£490 million
National infrastructure provider	£200 million
Logistics and transportation company	£30 million
Utility company	£30 million
International banking organization	£15 million
International insurer	£10 million
National infrastructure company	£9 million
Logistics and transportation company	£5 million

Yet Jones (ibid.) goes on to say that 'for very large and super large systems ... cancellations tend to exceed 50 per cent and the costs are enormous'. In 1996 the Standish group found that Fortune 100 companies cancelled 33 out of every 100 software projects, and ran over budget or beyond the deadline on another 40 (*Computer World*, 24 February 1997).

Isochron finds that 40–60 per cent of projects start with a negative net present value (NPV) and some actually have increased operating expenses on completion. Tom DeMarco (1982) suggested that only 15 per cent of information systems projects deliver useful results. Research by French-Thornton (quoted in *Computer Weekly*, 4 November 2003) reached a similar conclusion, reporting that 'only 16 per cent of projects come in on time, within budget, on schedule or meet scope' (which means, of course, that a massive 84 per cent do not).

Given this track record in which failures greatly outnumber successes it is a wonder that any company with sane management should ever embark on a large business change or IT project. However, the opportunities for success that do exist must not be missed. Failure can be prevented if the portfolio comprises well-chosen, well-managed projects that have, above all, been appraised with the objectives of the company foremost.

DEFINING THE PROJECT OBJECTIVES

Given the pessimistic statistics outlined above, it is apparent that any board contemplating the not inconsiderable expense of a new business change or IT project must focus on the expected benefits. Further, particular attention must be given to how those benefits will align with the strategy and objectives of the business. As all benefit forecasts must take risk and uncertainty into account, the board must be given the background to the calculations and know how much confidence can be placed in the project proposals. Financial appraisal methods, such as discounting cash flow forecasts to determine net present value, provide further evidence for the decision-maker. These considerations will be amplified in subsequent chapters, but here we introduce the basic parameters that will determine the ultimate failure or success of a project in terms of real benefits, in the place where the true benefits become apparent, namely in the company's accounts. These are the true value drivers.

A detailed checklist of possible benefit values is given in Chapter 3 in connection with establishing the business case for a single project (see Figure 3.2) but these benefits all fall within three main headings:

1. increased company share price and market valuation
2. increased *profitable* revenue from sales
3. reduction in operating costs and other cost savings, including sales of assets rendered unnecessary by the project.

These are the true tests against which each project proposal must be evaluated. They allow projects that may be quite different in their approach to change to be evaluated on a common basis. That, in turn, allows all project proposals to be compared on a like-for-like basis, which is essential when attempting to decide which projects should be given priority.

Bandwidth and the portfolio of projects

Suppose that, after evaluation of a number of project proposals, ten projects satisfy all the requirements and promise to yield valuable benefits that align with the company's objectives. However, most companies do not have unlimited funds or resources to commit to business change or IT projects. Quite apart from the financial investment needed, there is the question of resource bandwidth to consider. Communications engineers have long been familiar with this term as measure of frequency spread, but, for our purposes, resource bandwidth is used to express the organization's capacity in terms of people whose skills are key to its projects.

Isochron has found (and you can try this for yourself) that asking various project managers the question 'Which people are key to our work?' in each case produces a list of between 30 and 60 names (that is, 30 names for an SME and 60 for a large corporate). The lists will include the following:

- directors whose authority for sign-off or presence at meetings is essential
- administrators whose abilities or sanctions are fundamental to progress
- technical experts – for example, an Oracle database developer whose skills are unique.

It is the availability of these people to any project that constrains progress and *not* the total headcount of project workers.

Now consider that happens when our programme of ten simultaneous or overlapping projects is being considered for investment and authorization. If each of these projects would require the full-time attention of two IT experts from the organization's permanent staff, it is apparent that if only six suitably qualified IT professionals were to be employed, the maximum number of projects that could be started would be three. Even that proposition relies on all six of the IT people being available for all of the time, which in practice is never the case.

Even if there is sufficient budget and enough resource bandwidth to go ahead with all the projects that the organization would wish to, the impact of change on the day-to-day work of the business has to be considered. One of us was invited to look at the portfolio of projects planned for the modernization programme of a large government department. A simple analysis of the programme plan showed that some of the field offices of the department would be expected to implement as many as 12 significant changes *per month* in their working practices whilst maintaining normal services to the public. Given the time out needed for training, the disruption caused by new technology installation and the time needed to learn to work with new procedures, the programme plan was impossibly overambitious.

It is too easy to create impossible working conditions for people at the organization's 'coal faces'. A thorough impact analysis will often reveal that limited capacity to implement change is a further constraint on the size of the organization's project portfolio. Thus, because of budget, resource bandwidth and change impact an organization is rarely able to commission all the projects it would like to at any one time. It has to make decisions between them. On what basis can it do that? In a commercial company, the imperatives are usually profitability, shareholder value and regulatory compliance. In a public-sector organization the essentials are typically giving expression to policy and providing statutory services while maintaining value for money. In both cases these are usually expressed in terms of an organization's strategy. That strategy will often comprise:

- a mission statement
- strategic business objectives
- critical success factors (CSFs)
- key performance indicators (KPIs), perhaps linked to a balanced scorecard
- a strategic business plan, including unchanging basic principles and specific changes needed to deliver the strategic objectives
- high-level financial plans
- strategic risks.

These factors should (but do not always) link consistently into the plans for each business unit and to the departmental budgets.

Given that projects are the means by which a strategy is delivered, it is clearly both logical and essential that every project aligns with the strategic objectives (yes, we know this is repetition but the message is particularly important). If they are known, alignment should include the CSFs and KPIs. Further, if the projects are to be prioritized against each other they must be comparable on a like-for-like basis. Otherwise an organization will:

- carry out changes that it does not need and should not make
- fail to carry out parts of its strategy that it should.

An organization that directs its effort wrongly in these respects could be investing (or, rather, wasting) tens of millions, or even hundreds of millions, of pounds on inappropriate projects. Indeed, wastage has run to billions of pounds in a few public-sector IT projects. In an ideal world, a company's shareholders should be able to see how each and every project adds value to the shares in their pockets.

Figure 2.1 illustrates how one organization, using Isochron's methods, cleaned up and rationalized its projects portfolio. The statistics cover three years, but the improvement was apparent by the end of the first year. When the Isochron investigation started this company's success rate was 17 per cent, which is broadly in line with the general performance of IT and business change projects noted near the beginning of this chapter. By cutting out unprofitable projects, this company increased the probability of its project successes to 80 per cent over the three-year period measured, and it continues to benefit from its portfolio optimization. Asked to reflect on its own assessment of the reasons for this success, the company reported the following conclusions:

- The fall in the total number of projects in the portfolio for the year 2002–2003 was achieved by avoiding all projects that did not meet the overall objectives of

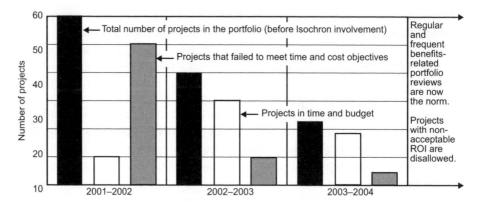

Figure 2.1   Project portfolio optimization in a company using Isochron's methods

the company's business plan (which included rejecting projects with a negative long-term return on investment (ROI) prediction.

- The further fall in portfolio content in 2003–2004 arose because the company's businesspeople were no longer even proposing projects that they knew would not meet the business plan and commercial objectives.

Reyck *et al.* (2005), in an interesting and well-researched article, cite additional evidence of the benefits of managing IT projects as an investment portfolio. However, in Isochron's view, the project portfolio should contain all the business projects because IT projects are only part of an organization's total investment package. IT projects should not be considered separately from business projects if investment decisions are to be made in the organization's best interests – as opposed only to the best interests of IT.

DOCUMENTING, COMMUNICATING AND USING THE PROJECT PORTFOLIO

Aligning the portfolio of projects requires, above all, a business strategy that is formally documented and communicated. A surprising number of organizations discuss their strategy but then either produce a strategy statement document that is unsuitable as a basis for project alignment or produce no documentation at all. There are several reasons why such documents are unsatisfactory. These include the following:

- The objectives are not clear or too vague in the text of the strategy statement.
- Proposed changes are mixed up with the strategic principles on which the company will operate.
- The principles themselves are not clearly stated.

We have also seen strategies where the business unit plans did not match the strategic business plan, and where the KPIs and CSFs did not align with (or even relate to) the strategic objectives. These failures usually arise because the task of creating the documentation has been delegated to a level where heads of business are operating in silos, or where the organization is so large that even senior managers have no understanding of their organization in the context of its market and competition.

In Isochron's experience, most employees in a private company are unlikely to have any awareness of the factors that drive the profitability or share value of their employer. They even fail to appreciate how important these issues are to their continuing security of employment.

Now assume instead that the strategic objectives, plans, CSFs, KPIs and risks have been correctly documented. This enables them to be set out in a table or used as input for analysis in a project portfolio tool. When that is done, the entire portfolio of projects (business and IT, large and small, initial idea to nearly complete) must be listed in the table – for reasons that will be made apparent in the following paragraphs.

We often come across organizations that are aligning and prioritizing only their larger IT projects. However *all* projects will use up fixed costs and resource bandwidth and have some impact on day-to-day operations. Thus, in these organizations, the smaller IT projects are pulling key and scarce resources away from the larger projects in an unplanned, and even unrecognized, fashion.

On analysis it will be found that some of the IT and many of the business projects have materialized through the personal initiatives of individual managers. Most, if not all, of these projects bear absolutely no relationship with company strategy. We are not suggesting that anything sinister is necessarily happening here. In most of these cases it is not that managers are deliberately spending their employer's money on personal schemes. Rather, it is just that a manager deeply immersed in the detailed workings of an organization tends to focus on immediate problems and the day-to-day needs of the job. So, an IT venture or change project that the individual manager considers would do something smarter or give better quality would appear at first sight to benefit the company, because the manager has fallen into the easy trap of failing to see the larger picture.

Uninformed peer pressure can lead managers into promoting unsuitable or even disastrous projects. In a survey of 615 senior executives carried out by the Chartered Management Institute, 40 per cent of managers felt that they had been led into making decisions against their better judgement by their peers and 20 per cent believed that lobbying by their colleagues has actually led them into making wrong project choices (see Gribben, 2005).

One of us (AF) was present at an awayday with his business team when the subject of team workload came up for discussion. A temporary and junior administrator was attending this meeting but was being entirely overlooked by the senior team members. Eventually the session leader turned to this junior administrator and asked, 'And do you have any observations to make?' Surprising everyone present, the administrator said, 'Yes I do. I've been watching all of you carefully and it seems to me that you are overperforming. You produce documents that nobody wants. You build them to a high standard that nobody needs. You are wasting much of your time that is needed urgently for other things.' Translate this into 'You are doing projects that nobody wants. You are using up resources that are urgently needed for other projects' and our point is made.

Identifying the entire project portfolio on one display for the first time can be a shock for senior management. It is quite common to find that the number of projects active in some stage or another is as much as ten times greater than people had thought! This is particularly true where there is no procedure for catching and assessing project ideas at the outset, no investment review system and no process that makes the whole picture visible to the executive. Taking stock of the project portfolio and getting it all assembled into a table in one place for the first time can be quite an expensive procedure. But the immediate cull of misaligned and inappropriate investments that usually follows shortly afterwards repays the effort many times over!

The projects portfolio can be gathered together using purpose-made portfolio software. Even a Microsoft Excel spreadsheet will often be quite adequate. Once this has been done, a procedure must be implemented to make sure that all new projects are added automatically to the portfolio in the future. A simple but very effective device is to ensure that a project that is not listed in the portfolio will get no budget to fund it (project authorization is described in Chapter 5). This needs to be backed up with an arrangement to ensure that the process is not circumvented by allowing senior managers to find money covertly from other budgets for projects that they particularly want to get done – which might happen even if those managers know that these are not projects that the company would allow if it knew about them. One of us (DL) remembers a small-scale, but particularly blatant, example of such backdoor project authorization, which is reported as Case 1 in Chapter 5.

The next consideration is to be able to compare project with project on a like-for-like basis. This requires some sort of scoring system in which each project's objectives can be scored according to the degree to which it matches with the strategic objectives, CSFs, KPIs and risks. It is, of course, important to avoid creating an industry of scoring and prioritizing that would use up costly and scarce resources that are needed actually to perform the projects. A subjective scoring process is quite enough, and the simpler it can be made the better.

Scoring projects on the basis of their best-estimated return on investment in budget and resources is trickier. It assumes that everyone who prepares estimates of benefits and costs for project business cases will do so on the same basis. It also assumes that double-counting of benefits and costs is eliminated. It was for these reasons that Isochron, in its development days, placed priority on creating a rigorous business case process, complete with a supporting software tool.

Many companies we have seen do not take ROI into account in prioritizing projects because they simply find it too hard to present figures that can be substantiated. There is too much scope for manipulation. However, if no attempt is made to find at least an indicative cash benefit value, there is a significant risk of confusing high cost of project with large value to the company. Indeed, one of us (AF) has been subjected to a serious attempt to argue that cost equates directly with value. In other words, the more we spend on our project the greater the value must be to our company!

CONCLUSION

In this chapter we have shown the importance of ensuring that every new project aligns with the organization's strategic objectives. A company needs to focus its investments on those projects that will return value, and this means creating and maintaining a project portfolio that allows projects to be selected and prioritized, taking into account bandwidth, other constraints, investment and benefit values. The use of one or more measures such as NPV, ROI, CSFs and KPIs must drive decisions on whether or not to proceed with a project and, by allowing like-for-like comparison, point to the appropriate project selection and prioritization decisions. These measures can be expected to result in a streamlined portfolio from which projects that have no chance of benefiting the business have been eliminated. Constant portfolio reviews will ensure that such wasteful projects stay eliminated.

Isochron has shown that the task of putting a cash value on benefits is not as difficult as many people think it has to be (see Chapter 3). However, the estimator must have a good understanding of the value drivers – the factors that drive the asset values, revenue and costs of the organization. The ability to carry out Monte Carlo analysis on estimates and present them as a Monte Carlo box is another necessity. These processes are part of preparing the business case, which is the subject of the next chapter.

REFERENCES AND FURTHER READING

DeMarco, T. (1982), *Controlling Software Projects*, Boston, MA: New Yourden Press.

Drucker, P. (1967), *The Effective Executive*, New York: HarperBusiness.

Gribben, R. (2005), 'Managers "Bounced" into Errors', in the jobs.telegraph.co.uk section of *The Daily Telegraph*, 17 November.

Holmes, A. (2001), *Failsafe IS Project Delivery*, Aldershot: Gower.

Jones, C. (1996), *Patterns in IT System Development Failure and Success*, Boston, MA: International Thomson Computer Press.

Reyck, B.D. *et al.* (2005), 'The Impact of Project Portfolio Management on Information Technology Projects' in *The International Journal of Project Management*, vol. 23, no. 7, October, pp. 526–37.

3 Making the Business Case

The business case, often introduced to the board or investors at a presentation meeting, should be embodied in a formal report document or presentation file because it will be needed not only when the case is first considered, but also frequently for future reference. The business case is often formulated by a single person or small expert group, but some emerge as a result of a long and expensive feasibility study undertaken by many people. Key elements of any business case are forecasts of return on investment and other quantifiable benefits that the project should generate (value), estimates of the associated costs, and an outline timescale for the significant events leading to project completion. Approval of a business case is not the end of the story because, once accepted, the business case becomes the one of the key components of the project charter or project initiation document (PID).

MORE THAN ONE BUSINESS CASE?

Suppose that a project is proposed that recommends a complete reorganization of a company, which would involve vacating some premises, building a new headquarters in Swindon, a huge IT investment, changing the numbers and kinds of staff employed and redirecting some tasks to outsourced providers offshore. But there might be other proposals under discussion at the same time. Why Swindon? Why not Exeter, or Edinburgh, or even somewhere overseas? How much, if anything, should be outsourced? Should the new organization be associated with a realignment of the company's target market?

Considering another example, imagine that a mining company has located valuable new copper ore deposits in South Africa in an area that already has some mineral processing capability. A project proposal has been made that includes not only sinking the new mineshaft, but also building a new copper refinery to replace the small refinery that already exists near the mine. But other proposals suggest that unrefined copper ingots might be moved by rail to an existing refinery in Zambia that has spare capacity. Yet another proposal suggests that the ingots should be shipped to a very efficient but underused refinery in South Africa. Such alternative strategies are commonly encountered in mining projects.

In a further example, the IT director (Pamela) of a large multinational group is aware that advances in computer technology and communications appear to have made possible many improvements in the commercial administration and business operations of individual companies within the group and over the group as a whole. Pamela regularly receives requests from the IT managers of group companies to sanction ambitious local improvement projects. She also has ideas of her own for projects that could have longer-term, wider impact across the whole group. Each of these projects, local and global, would need significant time and resources, but the group is currently short of cash and must be circumspect about committing new capital expenditure. The group board has, therefore, imposed an IT budget limit. It insists that Pamela prepares a formal business case for each of her own proposals, and she must ask each of the group company IT managers to do the same for their proposals.

In a large group there might be scores of proposals coming from several different companies. Different IT managers will have their own ideas about how to set out their proposals and about the relative benefits that their ideas would bring to their companies and the group. A commonsense rule when making any comparison, for business purposes or otherwise, is to attempt to present all the different cases according to a common or standard format, so that like can be prepared with like, apples with apples, pears with pears and dollars with dollars. Project and purchasing managers will be familiar with this concept from bid summary procedures, which attempt to bring proposals for a high-cost item from a diverse range of potential suppliers to a common base of date and total cost delivered at the point of use.

So, with business case proposals coming from so many different sources, a necessary but difficult task for Pamela is to insist that all the satellite IT managers prepare their proposals on a common basis, so that the board is more easily able to compare them and select those that will yield the greatest value to the business. This goes deeper than the method of presentation: all these IT managers must have a common appreciation of the processes that lead to sound estimates and business proposals, all of which will be easier to achieve if standard concepts and techniques are employed throughout. Isochron definitions and processes offer a simple approach that enables standardization.

After Pamela has filtered out the obvious non-runners there might still be a total of 20 new project proposals for submission to the group board. But now, with each having its own business case that sets out benefits, timing, costs and risks on a formal, standardized basis, the group board is better able to select the project or projects that will produce the best return on investment.

All these examples (there are countless others) illustrate that any proposal for a significant new project might give rise to a number of very different possible strategies, each of which would have its own associated timescale and estimate of costs and values. So if (say) five different strategies are investigated for a proposed new project, five different business cases must be made. That would mean repeating the procedures outlined in this chapter (and summarized in Figure 3.1) for each of those cases. When there is more than one possible business case for a single project,

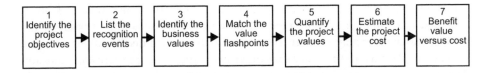

1 Identify the project objectives	2 List the recognition events	3 Identify the business values	4 Match the value flashpoints	5 Quantify the project values	6 Estimate the project cost	7 Benefit value versus cost

Figure 3.1   Seven important steps towards making the business case

or when there are a number of different project proposals in a company or group, the board is enabled not only to make a simple go or no-go decision for a new project, but is also able to select the case that should bring maximum benefit to the company by comparing all the options on a like-for-like basis.

HOW TO HIGHLIGHT THE BENEFITS – AND CONVINCE THE BOARD

An important prerequisite for the preparation of any business case (and, if accepted, its resulting project contract) is to define and quantify the objectives and scope of the proposed project. This process is often called project definition, but at this very early stage we prefer to call it project identification, not least because true project definition cannot be achieved until much later, when the project is completed and documented in its finished as-built and fully implemented state. Project identification must start by giving the proposed project a name and an outline description of its nature and purpose, with great emphasis on the project objectives.

Objectives versus solutions

Initially, projects should be defined in terms of their objectives. The extent to which those objectives are described provides a significant steer but, at the same time, a constraint upon the project manager in executing the project. Too often. definition of the objectives also provides a heavy indication of the preferred *how* things are to be done – rather than a specification of *what* is words, a physical solution is prescribed when the business case re be to define only the logical outcome. An overspecified objective manager's capability to explore pragmatic workarounds and alternatives that can meet the business's objectives in ways that are often found to be simpler, cheaper and faster to implement.

[handwritten annotation: how things are done Vs what is needed]

This argument can be illustrated by a very simple example. Consider the very commonplace process of paying suppliers' invoices. If that process is to be part of a new system, the relevant system objective should be labelled simply 'pay suppliers' invoices'. This is a *logical* description of the process; it is not *prescriptive*. It does not instruct the project manager to build in the actual physical method by which the suppliers have to be paid. Cash in plain brown envelopes, cheques, electronic funds transfer are just three of the possible ways of enacting this payment process. Provided that suppliers can be paid on time, all options should be open to the project manager. It may be that the project manager will decide to put a simple process in place as a temporary expedient, with the 'bells and whistles' solution following later. Using the simple invoice payment process might facilitate the early implementation of a wider-ranging system or set of processes, which would otherwise be delayed if the pragmatic temporary solution were excluded by an overdefined set of objectives. And that simple interim solution, although it might need greater clerical effort, could even prove to be the appropriate final solution when the costs of more complex alternatives are considered.

Isochron's objective transform approach (described below) concentrates on the objectives so that, with the 'how to do it' no longer set in stone, the project manager is given the flexibility to meet the project goals in whatever way works best within the timeframe. The business case should be concerned principally with setting out the expected benefit values, costs and timing of the project, all expressed in language that is familiar to the executives and investors who can either kill or breathe life into the project.

Project scope

A project scope statement sets out the portion or portions of the project that the company wishes to undertake and for which it is to be responsible.

When projects are carried out for external clients, responsibilities are often divided between the company, the client and others. For such projects, especially when they are contracted for a fixed price, project scope means defining the extent of the project for which the company is to be responsible (and for which it can expect to be paid). This is important for several reasons, including professional liability issues and to avoid payment disputes. Consider, for example, an IT project for an external client. Relevant questions might be as follows:

- How far is our company going to be responsible for implementing the system in the client's organization?
- What will our contractual obligations be for training the client's staff in operating the new systems, how far will that training go throughout the client's organization and are all those training costs allowed for in the project lump sum price?
- Do we have to provide operating manuals and, if so, in what languages?
- Will the client expect us to set up a continually manned problem hotline?

For internally funded projects the definition of scope has a somewhat different purpose. In this case the project is to be wholly owned by the company, and the company has ultimate responsibility for the entire project. Payment disputes owing to vague delineation of scope should not arise. Yet scope definition remains important, because if the outer limits of the project are not clearly declared the project manager's remit becomes ambiguous, with a risk that the project will stray far beyond its intended boundaries, budgets, timescale and effects. However, Isochron's objective transform approach automatically defines the intended project scope in terms of its objectives.

It is also helpful to set out key things that will lie outside the project scope, especially where these might otherwise have been considered as possibly being within it. To avoid further misunderstanding it may be useful to remind people of the focal purpose of the project.

Using objective transform technology

Objective transform is a technique developed by Isochron that translates sponsor and stakeholder aspirations into tangible, recognizable achievement goals. Briefed with these, project teams and business managers then find themselves with the task of making familiar and achievable things happen. Top-level milestones in project plans are stripped of technical jargon and become events that all business managers can easily understand and recognize. Those events, because they can more easily be translated into cash values, provide a focus for project management. An easy way to identify the events is to ask the project sponsor, 'How will you know/what will tell you when your expectations of this project are met?' Projects can then be organized and conducted according to the visible and final results that represent their true goals. Objective transform has two key elements. These are *recognition events* and *value flashpoints*.

Recognition events

Recognition events are somewhat similar to the project milestones with which all project managers and planners are familiar. A milestone is either achieved or not achieved. Its binary yes/no state allows no in-between possibility. This yes/no condition is important when measuring progress against a plan. If anyone working on a particular project task is asked to report the percentage completion of a task that is in progress, an answer such as 95 per cent can usually be taken with a fairly large pinch of salt because it is based on a subjective, usually optimistic, estimate. The only reliable indicators are:

1. The task has not been started.
2. The task has been started and is in progress.
3. The task is finished, meaning that the outcome has been observed and inspected, the result has been approved and the task has been completely put to bed.

Milestones, because they identify the third of these conditions, are valuable and totally reliable indicators of progress for the project manager. Thus far, recognition events and milestones are identical. However, recognition events are a special case because they have two important additional characteristics:

1. Recognition events signal to the project sponsor and principal stakeholders that one of their business objectives has been achieved. They are milestones of the ends, not the means.
2. Recognition events are driven by results and do not anticipate solutions. A milestone might be named 'Specification for new server released'. However, that is not a recognition event because it presupposes that a new server will be necessary and imposes a technical solution on the business case.

Here are a few examples of recognition events:

- first successful use of new system to make a new sale
- first staff save time by switching to new procedure
- first brochure issued to customers announcing discount for prompt payment
- the marketing department take occupation of the former machine room, avoiding new accommodation acquisition.

It is evident that each of these is an easily recognizable event that, when it happens, flags to the investors that the project has achieved one of their expectations.

Successful achievement of all recognition events will mean that the project objectives are achieved. Conversely, failure to achieve just one recognition event will disappoint the investors, the sponsor and the other stakeholders.

Value flashpoints

Value flashpoints comprise a special subset of recognition events. Each value flashpoint is a cash event that can be evaluated directly in monetary terms. Value flashpoints are used to map the project's financial implications to the overall business accounts. Examples include the following:

- payment, received into the accounts, arising from the sale of a relinquished property
- cessation of maintenance and leasing payments for equipment that has been released
- a stage payment received from the customer
- first receipts from the sale of a new product.

Each recognition event should be checked to see if it is, in fact, a cash event an event that can be seen in the accounts or in a financial report. If it is, then it should be defined as a value flashpoint. Achieving a value flashpoint is very important indeed to the sponsor and stakeholder of a business. It is hard evidence that all the foregoing project work has begun to pay off. It often marks the start of a value stream. The flashpoint itself is the turning point where a change to the status quo occurs; there may be a reduction in costs and similarly the expected benefits or penalties start to be realized.

Checklists are invaluable in many areas of project management, and the identification and generic analysis of possible project benefits is no exception. A fairly detailed (but not exhaustive) checklist which may help in the evaluation of benefits is given in Figure 3.2. Different organizations should develop lists specific to their own business needs for the guidance of personnel who are involved in building their business cases.

Value flashpoints become important controls after the business case has been approved and work on the project proceeds. Using value flashpoints, one can see precisely at each of the many times when progress is assessed whether or not an expected change to benefits is at risk or has begun. For example, a headcount reduction should be visible in the management accounts as being effective starting from its associated value flashpoint date. Value flashpoints make the tracking of benefits much easier.

When a value flashpoint in a programme of projects depends on two or more of those projects, it is important to divide and allocate its value in proportion to the contribution that each project is expected to make.

If a business case is assembled to support a go/no-go decision on a project, value flashpoints can greatly simplify comprehension. The numbers can more easily be interpreted and related to the calendar and the business objectives. For example, the release of two purchasing clerks in six months' time, vacating and ending all occupation and other expenses at our Chiswick branch at the end of the year, or first product sold on Monday 4 August 2008 are obvious benefits in which the values and their effective dates are clearly related.

Relationship between recognition events and value flashpoints

All value flashpoints are recognition events, but the converse is not true. Each value flashpoint must be a monetary event. The following are examples of recognition events that, although they will quite directly lead to a value flashpoint, are not in themselves recognizable events in the accounts or in a financial report:

1. The new office in Milton Keynes is ready for occupation.
2. The first of our new fleet of aircraft is delivered.
3. First implementation of simplified invoicing procedure.

Note that not even significant IT milestones such as the completion of user acceptance testing are recognition events, because they are not events that tell a sponsor that the business expectations of the project have been met.

There may be subtle distinctions that separate some recognition events from their associated value flashpoints. For example, relinquishing a property is an easily visible event, but the full benefits may only be realized some time later when the lease is terminated and all rental payments can cease. The event of ceasing to pay rent is of most interest, even though the move out of the building may be more visible.

Driver	Principal basis for evaluating benefits			
	Estimate of value expected from project	Multipliers		
Drivers that increase share price and company valuation: Positioning of the company in the acquisition/disposal market (see footnote)*	Difference between perceived company/ share valuation before and after news reaches the market	Company share valuation		
Profitable acquisition of new valuable personnel	Estimated sum competitors would pay to acquire the same potential new personnel	Number of personnel involved	Average acquisition cost difference	
Profitable enhancement of personnel value (depends how important credential is to the company)	Difference between acquisition value of personnel before and after their experience and training	Number of personnel involved	Average acquisition cost difference	
Profitable acquisition of intellectual capital (IC)	Estimated sum competitors would pay to acquire the same IC	Number of items of IC/personnel with IC involved	Average acquisition cost	
	Estimated market value of copyrights and patents	Number of copyrights and patents	Number of copyrights and patents	
	Estimated value of lost market consequent on successful application of know-how by competition, expressed as saving			
Profitable acquisition of brand	Estimated sum competitors would pay to acquire the brand	Number of brands involved	Average acquisition cost	
Profitable enhancement of brand	Difference between acquisition value of brand before and after enhancement	Number of brands involved	Average acquisition cost	
	Difference between estimated cost of errors traceable to lack of data/inaccessibility of data/erroneous data before and after enhancement of company data and knowledge	Difference in number of incidents before and after enhancement	Average cost of incident (see costs section below)	
Drivers that increase revenue: Increased volume of sales, driven by: Acquisition of new client relationships	Estimated value of revenue from named potential new clients	Number of new clients	Average client revenue	
Acquisition of new channels to market	Estimated value of revenue from named potential new clients through named new channels	Number of new clients	Average client revenue	
Development of products/services and the markets for them	Estimated value of revenue from potential new clients for potential new products/services and markets	Number of new products and services	Average client revenue	Number of new clients

Figure 3.2   A checklist of project benefit values (not exhaustive)

Acquisition of new sales personnel skills and relationships	Estimated value of revenue from potential new sales (identify clients and sales)	Number of new sales personnel	Average value of sales from each new salesperson
Acquisition of improved sales processes	Estimated value of revenue from potential new sales (identify clients and sales)	Number of new sales personnel	Average value of sales from each new salesperson
Acquisition of brand	Estimated value of revenue from named potential new clients from research into brand impact on buyers	Number of new clients	Average value of revenue per client
Enhancement of brand	Difference between estimated value of revenue from named potential new clients (from research into brand impact on buyers) before and after brand enhancement	Number of new clients	Average difference in value of revenue per client
Acquisition of new company data and knowledge	Estimated value of revenue from named potential new clients to be gained from analysis of new market and client data and knowledge	Number of new clients	Average value of revenue per client
Enhancement of value of company data and knowledge	Difference between estimated value of revenue from potential new clients to be gained from analysis of new market and client data before and after data enhancement	Number of new clients	Average difference in value of revenue per client
Faster adoption of changing technology	Estimated value of revenue gained from clients through being first to market	Number of new clients	Average value of revenue per client
Improved profit margin per sale, driven by: Better product/service alignment with market to optimize sales against price and cost	Difference between margin per sale before and (estimated) after realignment	Number of sales	Mode difference in margin per sale
Better pricing, driven by: Acquisition of new company data and knowledge on prices and costs	Difference between margin per sale before and (estimated) after acquisition of new company data and knowledge on prices and costs	Number of sales	Mode difference in margin per sale
Enhancement of value of company data and knowledge on prices and costs	Difference between margin per sale before and (estimated) after enhancement company data and knowledge on prices and costs	Number of sales	Mode difference in margin per sale
Income for sale of assets at more than book value: Sale of capital assets	Estimated value of capital assets to be sold	Number of sales of capital assets	Value of sales
Drivers that save or reduce costs: Reduced personnel costs, driven by: Reduced headcount	Value of payroll savings based on current and budgeted costs	Number leaving payroll	Payroll cost per person

Figure 3.2 *Continued*

	Estimated value of avoided recruitment costs	Number of new recruitments avoided	Cost (extended) of recruitment per person	
Reduced/avoided recruitment	Estimated value of avoided recruitment costs	Number of new recruitments avoided	Cost (extended) of recruitment per person	
Benefits	Value of payroll benefit costs (pensions, cars, etc., before and (estimated) after benefit reductions	Number of personnel affected	Reduction in cost of benefits per person	
Terms	Estimated cost of hours, holidays, etc. before and after changes in terms	Number of personnel affected	Reduction in cost or terms per person	
Accommodation	Cost of accommodation including overheads per square metre occupies before and after reductions in accommodation	Space given up in square metres	Accommodation cost per square metre	
Services	Cost of heat, light, power, catering before and (estimated) after personnel/accommodation changes. Note: avoid double-counting with reduced costs of capital assets.	Number of personnel/units of accommodation given up	Cost of services per person/per square metre of accommodation	
Training	Estimated value of training courses cancelled or avoided	Number of training courses cancelled or avoided	Average cost of training course	
Management and communications	Estimated value of opportunity cost of reduced time spent on management and communication	Notional cost per grade of personnel time and overheads	Amount of time released	Grade of personnel whose time is released
Skill-to-task mismatches	Estimated value of opportunity cost of reduction in time spent on: (1) consequences of choosing suboptimal approaches to work; (2) skills transfer; (3) rectification of errors; (4) 'wrong first time' work	Notional cost per grade of personnel time and overheads	Amount of time released	Grade of personnel whose time is released
Reduced costs of managing capital assets driven by: Reduced maintenance costs	Difference in value of maintenance costs before and (estimated) after contract changes or release of assets	Costs saved per asset/period	Number of assets involved	Period of calculated saving
Reduced security costs (including losses)	Difference in value of cost of damage and losses before and (estimated) after changes in contracts or release of assets	Cost of damage/loss per asset/period		Period of calculated saving
Reduced insurance costs	Difference in value of insurance costs before and after changes in contracts or release of assets	Cost of insurance per asset/period	Difference in number of assets involved	Period of calculated saving

Figure 3.2   *Continued*

	Difference			
Reduced costs of research and development (R&D), driven by:				
Reduced length of R&D cycle	Difference in whole life cycle cost of R&D projects before and (estimated) after change	Average cost of R&D life cycle	Number of R&D life cycles	
Better use of company data and knowledge	Difference between estimated value of R&D output before and after improved use of company data and knowledge	Value of R&D output per R&D project	Number of R&D projects	
Reduced costs of production, driven by:				
Reduced costs of raw materials	Difference between average costs of raw materials before and (estimated) after procurement changes	Average cost of raw materials		
Reduced costs of tools and machinery	Difference between development, implementation and servicing costs of tools and machinery before and (estimated) after changes	Average cost of raw materials		
Reduced costs from improved process efficiency	Difference between cost per unit of output before and (estimated) after process improvement	Average cost per unit output	Number of unit outputs	
Reduced cost of sales, driven by:				
Reduced sales effort per sale	Difference between sales effort (translated to notional cost) before and after changed sales procedures	Average staff hours per sale	Notional cost per staff hour	Average overhead costs per sale
Reduced volume of unprofitable sales	Difference in number of unprofitable sales before and after changed guidance or changed products/services	Average loss per sale	Average number of unprofitable sales	Period of calculated saving
Reduced costs of projects, driven by:				
Reduced/avoided/cancelled purchases	Difference between planned/budgeted/committed expenditure on purchases before and after reduction/avoidance/cancellation	Number of planned /budgeted /committed purchases	Average cost per purchase	Or known cost of purchases
Reduced/avoided third-party costs	Difference between planned/budgeted/committed expenditure on purchases before and after reduction/avoidance/cancellation	Number of planned /budgeted /committed contracts	Average cost per contract	Or known cost of contracts
Reduced/avoided opportunity costs	Difference between planned/committd/budgeted expenditure on internal staff costs including overheads before and after redeployment	Man-days of staff time redeployable	Average cost per man-day including overheads	Percentage of lost opportunity cost

Figure 3.2 *Continued*

Reduced costs of capital, driven by: Reduced inventory	Difference between value of inventory including warehouse overheads before and after reduction	Average cost per inventory item including overheads	Number of items eliminated from stock	Notional cost of capital
Reduced work in progress (WIP)	Difference in WIP before and after changes in invoicing and cash collection/debt recovery processes and/or billing styles	Average value of WIP		
Reduced debtors	Difference in value of debt before and after changes in cash collection/debt recovery processes	Average value of debt per day	Number of days debt outstanding	Notional cost of capital
Reduced costs of rectification, driven by: Reduced effort per error on investigation and recovery	Difference between internal staff costs spent on investigating and recovering errors before and after changes in quality assurance/quality control and/or data holding, availability and quality	Man-days of staff time redeployable	Average cost per man-day including overheads	Percentage of lost opportunity cost
Reduced volume of re-supply per error	Cost of re-supply operations before and after changes in quality assurance/quality control and/or data holding, availability and quality	Average cost of a re-supply operation	Average number of re-supply operations	Period of calculated saving
Reduced billing write-offs/compensation per error	Cost of billing write-offs/compensation before and after changes in quality assurance/quality control and/or data holding, availability and quality	Average cost of a write-off or compensation	Average number of write-offs or compensation events	Period of calculated saving
Reduced legal expenditure per error	Possible change in cost of indemnity insurance before and after changes in quality assurance/quality control and/or data holding, availability and quality	Cost of indemnity insurance		Period of calculated saving

Figure 3.2   Concluded

A test of relevance for a recognition event is whether one can identify the value flashpoint to which it contributes; if it cannot be associated the merits of its inclusion in the business plan should be seriously questioned. For example, the press announcement of a new product release is a recognition event that may not in itself generate value, but it is directly associated with taking orders for this new product. Revenue from the first orders is the value flashpoint in this case.

Most value flashpoints will follow a series of recognition events, but some might stand alone. Value flashpoints can occur early in a project, certainly before any IT is complete and delivered. For example, a business may be able to renegotiate procurement contracts in advance of its new electronic procure-to-pay system, thus helping to sustain purchases through those new contracts. Occasional 'flashes of lightning' can generate immediate cash value. Such flashpoints include what are often referred to as 'quick wins'. This theme is continued in Chapter 4 (see, particularly, Figure 4.1 in this context).

Relationship between objectives and value flashpoints

Each business objective for the project must have at least one clearly identifiable event that produces benefits. If a proposed objective cannot be dissected in that manner, then the objective itself should be questioned. If the events that flag achievement of the objective cannot be recognized, project management is not possible.

It is important that the emphasis is kept upon visible business benefits and not on the intermediate deliverables (even though these may be essential parts of the plan). For example, the implementation of a new computer system would have no meaning to the business executive, unless it can be designated as a milestone leading directly to a significant reduction in costs – a value flashpoint.

Put 'We are increasing our server capacity to 100 gigabytes' as an objective in the business plan and watch the collective eyes of the board glaze over. A slightly better approach might be to say that 'The average the time taken to answer enquiries from potential new customers will be reduced from ten minutes to one minute'. Even so, we can still imagine at least one sceptical board member responding with 'So what?'. 'The proposed project will increase new customer take-up from the current 20 per cent of enquiries to 25 per cent' might be better. Or why not say 'The new project will bring in 1000 new customers'? But, if you really want to grab the attention of all the directors put 'The 1000 new customers generated by this project will produce a return on investment of 20 per cent and increase our annual profit before tax by £100 000'. Now those are the real business objectives. These are the project objectives that the business plan should have stated up-front, together with an explanation of how they can be recognized when they are achieved. Then, of course, you must be able to explain how this project is going to bring all this about. Increasing server capacity may prove to be a technological necessity within just one of several different solutions.

Value flashpoints register

The business case for a large project will usually identify a number of value flashpoints and it is simplest to set these out in a table or register, an example of which is given in Figure 3.3. There is no need to 'overengineer' this step.

Until the first value flashpoint occurs, the project has not started to deliver any return on the funds invested. Further, the project cannot be considered as finished until all the value flashpoints have been achieved. This is a radical change of thought for people who have been brought up to feel that a project is finished as soon as the IT department have transferred responsibility for a new system to the business. At a stroke it incorporates 'business readiness' into the heart of the project.

Objective transform as an aid to better communication

The identification of recognition events and value flashpoints has great benefit in communication across the project organization, especially where cross-functional teams are involved. By carefully expressing each event in terms that businesspeople can associate with, project jargon is replaced by language that is more easily and universally understood. For example 'PID signed off' promotes far less common understanding than 'first sample of new product shipped to pilot customers'. At the same time, use of recognition events and value flashpoints enhances expression of the plan and its current status to external stakeholders. Often it can be beneficial to create a wallchart showing just these events against a timeline, leaving out all the technological events which, although they might impress, would certainly confuse the sponsor.

If you communicate the recognition events and value flashpoints across the project and stakeholder community you will find that everyone becomes directed towards the same project outcome. For example, a finance company was concerned that its employees should comply with money laundering legislation. The company made a video that showed, among other things, a suspect investment in a start-up company. After watching this video, the employees realized that they would need to scrutinize small company investments from a new perspective and with additional care.

ESTIMATING THE BENEFITS

When all the value flashpoints have been identified and listed, the task of benefit evaluation and cost estimating can begin. Every project is expected to produce some benefits: otherwise it should not be undertaken. However, the nature and extent of those benefits is not always easy to determine at the outset. A project intended to launch a new product would, for example, be expected (through eventual sales of the product) to bring increased revenues and profit. There are usually other intangible benefits or side effects that are less easy to predict and difficult to evaluate, although with determination it is usually possible to put a value on all of them (see the first section of Figure 3.2). Even regulatory imperatives can usefully have a cash value put on them, such as:

- What is the cost of fines avoided?
- What is the value of doing the project now, rather that at the eleventh hour?

Estimating the tangible benefits

The value to the business of tangible project outcomes can be estimated by logical deduction, often assisted by using well-established procedures. For example, if it is intended to relocate a company's headquarters in a new, cost-efficient building one mile away from the existing headquarters, simple arithmetical comparisons between the costs of maintaining and managing the two different buildings should indicate reliably the immediate benefits to the business when the value flashpoint 'accommodation costs on old building cease' is reached.

Simple arithmetic and established procedures will not always result in reliable estimates because the parameters are often uncertain. For example, a company with a long history of manufacturing cosmetics should be able to estimate fairly accurately how much it would cost to design, make and launch a new product. But the costs of manufacture will be dependent on the production quantities and that, in turn, will depend on the volume of sales that can be achieved. Market research and previous experience with own-brand products would seem to be reliable indicators. So the company should be able to make its sales forecasts, profit predictions and return-on-investment calculations with confidence. But markets are fickle and subject to sudden and unexplained change, and there are several instances of products that have had to be withdrawn simply because they did not appeal to the buying public as expected. However, the tangible benefits of most projects can be estimated with some degree of confidence using the Monte Carlo approach (see 'Monte Carlo Analysis, below).

Estimating the intangible benefits

Many benefits expressed in a business case have intangible value, especially when the project is for a business change. Goodwill and intellectual property rights are two examples of intangible assets that are familiar to accountants. The relationship between tangible and intangible benefits can be demonstrated using a typical (but entirely fictional) case example.

Wonderful Widgets plc occupies a large listed building in the centre of London and wishes to replace its inefficient mix of central heating and local air-conditioning

VALUE FLASHPOINT REGISTER

Project: Re-engineering of Commercial Division
Strategic agenda: The implicit agenda is to improve shareholder asset value and share price
Strategic objective: Re-engineer Commercial Division units to deliver a net reduction in costs of £25 million over 5 years
Programme objective: Re-engineer Commercial Division units to deliver a net improvement in P&L of £12.5 million over 2 years

Project objective	Value flashpoint	Estimated value of benefit stream (using Monte Carlo box and factoring risk)	Recognition events • How will you know? • What will you tell you when?	Date	Location	Observer	Context of event
Reduce retail costs	First member of retail staff leaves the payroll	£1.0 million over three years	First member of retail staff leaves the payroll	17Apr09	Allandale building	John Smith, CFM	Operational review meeting
			First retail outlet starts to operate in new way	9Jan09	Wending branch	Herbert Johnson, Retail Manager	Branch visit
			First outlet uses new IT in business to enable new way of operating	5Jan09	Wending branch	Herbert Johnson, Retail Manager	Branch visit
Reduce billing delays	First weekly report shows improvement in trailing days	£2.5 million over two years	First weekly report shows improvement in trailing days	24Jul09	Head Office Finance Dept.	John Smith, CFM	Operational review meeting
			First billing based on provisional data	15Nov08	Allandale building	John Smith, CFM	Project steering committee meeting
			First customer receives new style of call service from call agent	5Dec08	Newford customer contact centre	Marlene Johnson, Call Centre Manager	Call analysis
			First billing run with bill notes payment within 14 days	17Feb09	IT Centre, Sleedale building	George Potts, IT Director	Billing run
			First brochure issued promising discounts for prompt payment	7Nov08	Allandale building	Jane Dorman, Marketing Manager	Promotion
Reduce IT service charges	First member of IT staff leaves payroll	£2.5 million over 18 months	First member of IT staff leaves Payroll	30Sep09	Allandale building	John Smith, CFM	Operational review meeting
			Contract placed with outside service provider	10Jul09	Allandale building	Peter Wylie, Procurement Manager	Contract acceptance

Figure 3.3   A value flashpoint register

Objective	Benefit milestone	Benefit value	Event	Date	Location	Owner	Activity
Reduce call demand to the call centre	First member of call centre staff to be made redundant leaves the payroll	£2.0 million over two years	First member of call centre staff to be made redundant leaves the payroll	30Oct09	Head Office Finance Dept.	John Smith, CFM	Operational review meeting
			First product line relaunch with simplified features	14Jan09	Allandale building	Jane Dorman, Marketing Director	Promotion
			First billing run with new simplified and clarified bill notes	16Feb09	IT Centre Sleedale building	George Potts, IT Director	Billing run
			Query volume in call centre reduces	27Mar09	Newford customer contact centre	Marlene Johnson, Call Centre Manager	Weekly statistics review
			Reduction in measured workload	13Apr09	Newford customer contact centre	Marlene Johnson, Call Centre Manager	Weekly statistics review
Reduce the variety of product schemes	First member of customer services staff made redundant leaves the payroll	£3.0 million over two years	First member of customer services staff made redundant leaves the payroll	30Nov09	Head Office Finance Dept.	John Smith, CFM	Operational review meeting
			First product scheme withdrawn from brochures and outlets	9Dec09	Allandale building	Jane Dorman, Marketing Director	Operational review meeting
			Last purchase of product scheme occurs	13Apr09	Allandale building	James Peters, Ops. Director	Operational review meeting
			Customer service and retail workload reduces	15Jun09	Stopford	John Harbin, Head of CS	Monthly dept. meeting
Centralize customer services in one building	Cash from sale transfer reaches company accounts	£1.5 million in second year	Cash from sale transfer reaches company accounts	12Mar10	Head Office Finance Dept.	John Smith, CFM	Weekly accounts report check
			Removal firm completes removal contract leaves the building	10Apr09	High Heath House	Harry Green, Estates Manager	Contract completion check
			Last refurbishment contractor finishes work and leaves building	30Sep09	High Heath House	Harry Green, Estates Manager	Contract completion check
			Agents appointed	9Oct09	Allandale building	Peter Wylie, Procurement Mgr.	Contract acceptance
			Security and maintenance contractors arrive	16Oct09	High Heath House	Harry Green, Estates Manager	Work briefing
			Property advertised	16Nov09	Allandale building	Harry Green, Estates Manager	Contract progress review
			Purchase contract completed	8Jan10	Allandale building	Peter Wylie, Procurement Mgr.	Communication with agent

Figure 3.3   Concluded

units with a centralized, energy-saving climate control system. The tangible benefits foreseen include a reduction in overall energy costs of £50 000 per annum, starting from the day when the new system is declared fully functional (a value flashpoint). The system will cost a total of £500 000, payable in instalments to Fraish Aire Limited, who are to be the only contractor involved (payment of each instalment will be a value flashpoint for Fraish Aire Limited).

There are further benefits that *seem* to be intangible and often these are staff-related. The most significant is avoidance of threatened industrial action: the trade union involved has agreed to call off an impending strike on the understanding that the working environment will be improved. So, one benefit of the new project is going to be the amount of money saved in avoiding the disruption caused by the strike, which can easily be estimated in monetary terms. Further benefits should be observable at Wonderful Widgets months, or even years, after the project has been completed. These can include reduction in staff turnover, improved productivity and a general improvement in staff morale, all because the workforce now have a better working environment and a feeling that senior management care about them and their working conditions. With some imagination all of these benefits can be evaluated, either directly or by comparing current employment costs with the costs measured just before the new environmental controls were introduced. A value flashpoint is reached on each occasion when such benefits can be measured and assessed.

Accounting practice has a strict definition for 'intangible value'. Projects can bring about such benefits and they can have monetary values. To explain, consider what happens at Fraish Aire Limited, who will be conducting this project primarily for a trading profit – a tangible benefit that can be forecast and measured by long-established procedures. From Fraish Aire's point of view, each receipt of a stage payment is a value flashpoint. Now suppose that, as a result of designing this project for Wonderful Widgets, Fraish Aire has developed a novel and particularly efficient design for a heat exchanger element. This will forthwith have the registered trademark Fraishchange, and the company has applied for (and expects to be granted) international patents. These intellectual property rights have an intangible value. The best way of evaluating the patent rights is to estimate how much another company might be prepared to pay for a licence to make and sell the product.

If one or both companies derive benefit from the project, and their stock market values are enhanced as a direct result, the increase in goodwill (an intangible benefit) can be calculated by the accountants. The goodwill of each company is defined as the excess of the stock market valuation of the company over the value of the net assets shown in the balance sheet, a difference that represents, in monetary terms, the company's trading advantages and reputation.

Uncertainty in benefit estimating

A method for dealing with uncertainty in estimates, which greatly assists decision-making at the project go/no-go stage, is to calculate the probability or degree of confidence that can be placed in the estimates. This method, Monte Carlo analysis, is also invaluable for calculating probable cost estimate values. It is more widely used in assessing the probability of completing projects on time, but that use relates more to manufacturing and construction projects than to business change projects because, when business changes are managed by the Isochron methodology, times are deterministic and fixed.

Some uncertainties are not directly connected with the estimating method or the competence of the estimators but relate to the amount of risk to which the project is subject. Some risks have to be borne. The pharmaceutical industry, for example, is awash with instances of projects to produce and sell new drugs that have failed disastrously when, following a period of apparent success, previously unsuspected side effects cause panic among patients and the various regulatory authorities. Risk analysis and management are described briefly in Chapter 6, but the risk assessment process should start from the project beginning and be reviewed constantly as the project proceeds. The most significant risks are those that threaten to affect the value flashpoints.

Monte Carlo analysis

When Monte Carlo analysis is used, the project benefits should be estimated first. The benefits must have priority because they are the primary justification for contemplating investment in the project. If the benefits analysis appears promising, then the effort of analysing project costs becomes justified.

The first step in a Monte Carlo analysis is for the estimator to consider each value flashpoint and, in addition to his or her first estimate, add a highest possible value and a lowest possible value. When estimating an 'unknown' figure, it helps to set the highest and lowest boundaries first. This makes it easier to be comfortable with the best estimate.

1. Estimate the lowest value that the benefit (or cost) could have. Note that a low benefit limit could, in extreme cases, even be a negative value, indicating a possibility that the project could make things worse.
2. Estimate the highest value that the benefit (or cost) could have. For example, savings in procurement costs could never exceed the total procurement cost budget or even a large fraction of it.
3. Estimate the most likely value.
4. Estimate risk based on past performance of benefit realization. Factor in double-counting, which means taking into account other projects necessary to achieve the value flashpoint.

There might be some difficulty in using a commercially available project management package to perform Monte Carlo analysis, because all such software developers assume that their product will be used in an organization that employs at least one qualified and experienced project manager and not least a project support office staffed with experienced planning and cost engineers. However, many business change projects are carried out in companies which have no experienced project management staff and, further, have no general need for them. Recognizing the need of such organizations the Isochron approach, far from relying on the use of professional project managers, actively discourages allowing sophisticated project management systems to dominate the project management process. Isochron has a user-friendly, simplified approach to Monte Carlo analysis that any competent business manager can understand and use. It requires only figures that are already available in most organizations' accounts. Although more complex approaches and tools can be used, Isochron believes that the greater invested effort required for them is disproportionate to the value of the improvement in the estimate.

Uncertainty in cost estimating

To minimize uncertainty, costs should be estimated, as far as possible, according to the following principles:

1. Use detailed checklists to reduce the risk of omissions.
2. Use the best possible source. Business change projects do not have the advantage of construction projects in this respect, because there are no published tables. Wherever feasible, the managers and finance staff who will be responsible for the project work should be involved in making the estimates and should be committed to the resulting budgets. The use of value flashpoints will facilitate their involvement.
3. Examine any available cost data from similar previous projects.
4. Use accepted (traditional) project cost estimating methods. See, for example Lock (2003) or Roetzheim and Beasley (1997).
5. Consider, and take account of, risks, again wherever possible taking account of previous experience from whatever sources are available. Factor in your track record of cost management.

Figure 3.4 is an example of a checklist for a business change project. A document such as this is useful as a reminder of all the activities that have to be conducted and it will help to prevent errors of omission during cost estimating. The list is set out in a hierarchical structure, and all items have been allocated codes that could be used later in a management information or cost accounting system. Coding systems should be kept as simple as possible, but a well-designed code of accounts will allow analysis and reporting of project costs against budgets.

Code/category/subcategory/cost element		Code/category/subcategory/cost element	
010000	Business analysis	030201	Other contributions to central funds
010100	Business redesign	030300	Project administration
010101	Major process procedures design	030301	Project accounting
010102	IS procedures design	030302	Resource management
010103	Data model design (logical)	030303	Project facilities management
010104	Report and MI design	030304	General administration
010105	Develop procedures documentation	030400	Project management
010200	Current state assessment	030401	Project structuring
010201	Information systems review	030402	Project planning
010202	Use organization assessment	030403	Project control
010203	Process assessment	030404	Project monitoring
010204	Reporting and MI assessment	030405	Issue management
020000	Business change	030406	Change management
020100	Business user training	030407	Project reporting
020101	Identify communities to be trained	030408	Travel
020102	Conduct training needs analysis	030409	Hotel
020103	Develop training plan	030410	Subsistence
020104	Develop training course material	040000	Technology solution
020105	Schedule training events	040100	Applications support
020106	Administer training events	040101	Design support model
020107	Deliver training courses	040102	User environment design
020108	Monitor training feedback	040103	IS environment design
020200	Communications	040104	Procedures design
020201	Identify communication audiences	040105	Training design
020202	Develop communication strategy	040106	Implement support model
020203	Select communication media	040107	Monitor support services
020204	Develop communication plan	040200	Custom development
020205	Implement communication plan	040201	Application infrastructure devpmt.
020206	Assess audience understanding of key message	040202	Business system design
		040203	Testing design
020207	Update communication plan	040204	Data conversion application devpmt.
020300	Project contract development	040205	Application software development
020301	Identify objectives	040206	System testing
020302	Identify event milestones	040207	Implementation planning
020303	Identify business values	040300	Hardware
020304	Match flashpoints to value drivers	040301	Servers
020305	Quantify values	040302	Clients
020306	Determine project cost	040303	Connectivity
020307	Balance value against cost	040304	Peripherals
020308	Develop project contract	040400	Implementation
020309	Obtain approval	040401	Data conversion
020400	Stakeholder management	040402	Acceptance testing
020401	Develop stakeholder management plan	040203	Installation of production system
		040204	Refine production system
020402	Implement stakeholder management plan	040205	Evolution planning
		040300	Package integration and testing
020403	Stakeholder analysis	040301	Installation and environment set-up
020404	Develop stakeholder role transformation plan	040302	Package integration design and pilot
		040303	Package business system design
020405	Implement stakeholder role transformation plan	040304	Package application development
		040304	Package integration testing design
020406	Manage stakeholder issues	040305	Data conversion application dvpmt.
020407	Integrate stakeholder management and communication plans	040306	System testing
		040307	Implementation planning
030000	Project running costs	040400	Package selection
030100	Facilities	040401	Package requirements analysis
030101	Accommodation charges	040402	Vendor and package screening
030102	IT charges	040403	Package shortlist evaluation
030103	Room hire	040404	Final evaluation and selection
030104	Food and refreshments	040405	Contracts and technology acquisition
030105	Printing and stationery	040406	Development planning
030200	Overhead allocations	040407	Licences

Figure 3.4   A project activity and cost estimating checklist (not exhaustive)

Inevitably the cost estimate will contain uncertain elements because almost every cost estimate can only be a matter of judgement or best guess. Therefore cost estimates must be subjected to the same Monte Carlo analysis method as that used to assess the probability of benefits estimates. This helps to ensure the same granularity in benefit and cost estimates.

There are various ways of attempting to offset estimating errors and omissions, the most common of which is the addition of a contingency allowance for the total project (often called a below-the-line allowance because it is shown on the estimate tabulation below a line drawn under the prime cost total). However, contingency allowances are subject to Parkinson's Law (Parkinson, 1958), and contingency work is apt to be allowed to fill the contingency time known to be available. Contingency allowances have to be kept low and controlled if the forecast return on project investment is not to be completely eroded.

When the project duration and cost inflation rates would lead to increased costs in later years, an escalation allowance must be added as another below-the-line item.

INTRODUCING THE DIMENSION OF TIME

Time, costs and values are related in several ways. For example, if one were given the opportunity of undertaking a project costing a safe £10 million at a guaranteed fixed price of £20 million, but with the entire price to be paid six months after project completion, most individuals would be unable to take up the challenge through lack of immediate funds. So all recognition points and, most importantly, all the value flashpoints have to be set in a timeframe. This can be done only as an outline summary plan when making the business case, but we should use the backcasting method described in Chapter 4,

The cash outflows of any project are linked to the work and purchases needed to bring about the value flashpoints that occur throughout the project life cycle. It is generally well known that costs start to rise at a low rate when the project starts, build to a high rate during the main period of project execution, and then tail off as the project nears completion and ends. Figure 3.5 shows the general pattern of cash outflows, always known as an 'S' curve to project managers and cost engineers. The example in Figure 3.5 is smoothed, but in practice the curve will be jagged as various high-cost events occur.

The cash outflow patterns for both Fraish Aire and Wonderful Widgets should follow the general 'S' curve shape shown in Figure 3.5, but with some important differences. The cash outflow events for Wonderful Widgets will be triggered solely by stage payments made to Fraish Air. Wonderful Widgets can expect no benefits until after the project has been completed and commissioned, so the Wonderful Widgets accountants must make certain that sufficient funds are available for all the project costs. Fraish Air should be in a far better net cash flow position because the company can expect to receive stage payments from Wonderful Widgets to offset its expenditure during the course of the project.

So, if each company sets out all its value flashpoints on a timescale, using both inflows and outflows to derive the net flows, the net cash position of Wonderful Widgets will remain in the red until after project completion, and it is only when the value flashpoints occur and cash benefits start to accrue that the initial investment

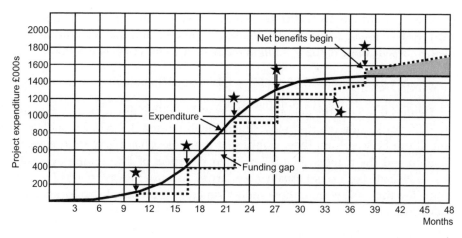

Figure 3.5   Cash outflow pattern for a project with value flashpoints superimposed

will be recovered. Indeed, it is a general characteristic of successful business change projects that the project costs will outstrip the benefits by a wide margin on initial project completion. The benefits will be realized subsequently, both as single value flashpoint events and as a continuing stream of enhanced cash inflows (through increased revenues and cost savings). That condition is depicted in Figure 3.5. The true end of a business change project is not when the new systems are introduced (and, all too often, the project team is disbanded) but when the last of the value flashpoints has been realized and all the new value streams have begun. Just as a mechanical project goes into an operation and maintenance phase after completion, so the changes introduced by a business change project must be maintained if the benefits are to be sustained and built upon.

Net present value

For many short-term projects, the time when the accrued cash benefits match and pass the original investment determines the so-called 'breakeven point' at the end of the payback period. Different finance departments in different organizations and markets seek different payback periods. In a fast-moving retail market, payback is usually sought within 18 months or less. In utilities, with their costly infrastructure investments, payback is usually required within five to ten years. For these projects with longer payback periods, the relationship between each cash flow item and the time of its occurrence must be taken into account. It is here that we need to introduce the concept of net present value.

Every dollar or pound paid into our bank today is worth more to us than a dollar or pound received at some future date. To illustrate this, take the example of a debt of £1 million pounds that has fallen due for payment today but the debtor cannot pay until one year's time. Suppose that our current expectation of return on investment is 5 per cent per annum. If that £1 million does eventually reach our bank in 12 months' time its effective value to us will be 5 per cent less than if it had been received today. So we can determine, in a process known as discounting, that the net present value of the £1 million received in a year's time is as follows:

Net present value (NPV) = £(1 × 1/1.05) = £0.95 million

Figure 3.6 sets out the net present values of £1 million discounted over periods up to 20 years using return-on-investment (ROI) rates of 2.5, 5.0, 7.5 and 10 per cent. It can be seen from these graphs that if a project has a very short expected duration and the required ROI is low, then the effect of discounting over short periods is small. So, it is not usually necessary to discount the cash flows of projects lasting less than one year. In those short-term projects the simple payback method is adequate.

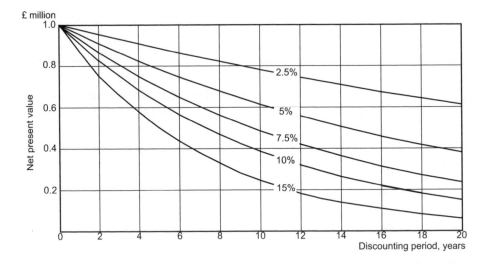

Figure 3.6   Net present value of £1 million discounted over 20 years

When a project has a mix of costs and benefits spread out over several future years, the cash inflows and outflows must be tabulated against a timescale so that each cost or benefit is placed in the period to which it belongs (years are the customary periods). When Isochron's objective transform technique is used, the dates of the value flashpoints (and the starts of continuing value streams) are already determined by the project sponsor. In each period the costs and benefits are compared or, rather, the outflows are subtracted from the inflows. That gives the forecast net cash flow for each period, with positive values representing net inflows and negative values denoting net outflows. Each period's net cash flow must next be discounted by the appropriate factor, which is determined by the time delay and required rate of return on investment. Figure 3.7, a once-popular proforma, is still useful for this illustrating this process, Discount factors used to be obtainable from published tables; now they can either be obtained easily from a pocket calculator, or a computer program such as Microsoft Excel can perform and tabulate the whole job.

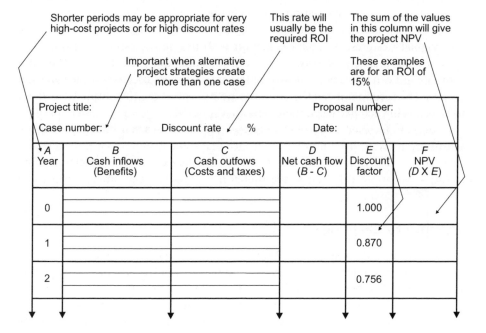

Figure 3.7   Upper portion of a proforma for calculating the net present value of a project

The calculation is carried forward for as many periods as the project is expected to remain viable, and the project NPV is found by adding all the period NPVs. A negative result indicates that, on the basis of all the estimated figures, the project will fail to achieve the required rate of return on investment. A positive NPV is an indicator that the project should be approved. An NPV of zero means that the rate of return for the project is likely to be exactly at the required level. Note that a project may have a negative NPV yet still be authorized to go ahead. The work may be justified for its intangible benefits, such as goodwill and so on.

Every business case rests on the degree of confidence that can be placed on all the parameters used in the net present value computations. No one should advocate investment in a new project before some attempt has been made to reduce the degree of uncertainty to reasonable proportions. One step in this direction, mentioned above, is to add a contingency allowance below the bottom line of the estimate. However, this does not answer the question of uncertainties in estimating the project benefits. Two methods are commonly used – Monte Carlo analysis (already described above) and sensitivity analysis.

Sensitivity analysis

Before starting a sensitivity analysis, the accountant or business analyst must carry out a net present value computation using the discounted cash flow method outlined in the preceding section of this chapter.

Sensitivity analysis can then proceed. The analysis consists simply of repeating the original net present value calculation with one of the estimated parameters increased or reduced by (say) 5 per cent. Numerous reiterations of the NPV computation can be carried out with different parameters selected for the variation process. The accountant can then discover how sensitive the NPV evaluation would be to errors in each particular parameter that is tested.

The risks factored into the benefit and cost estimates can be analysed using sensitivity analysis. It is important to notice that some risks have far more leverage than others: in other words, the estimates are likely to be considerably more sensitive to certain risks. These are therefore among the high-impact risks to be discussed in Chapter 6.

The Monte Carlo box

When Monte Carlo analysis has been used, the detailed histograms and graphs typically produced by most commercial packages are not the best way of presenting the results in the business case for the board or principal investors to consider. The simplified approach to Monte Carlo advocated by Isochron for the business analyst or project director produces a much clearer Monte Carlo box chart along the lines of that shown in Figure 3.8, in which both benefit and cost predictions are summarized together. The chart is self-explanatory.

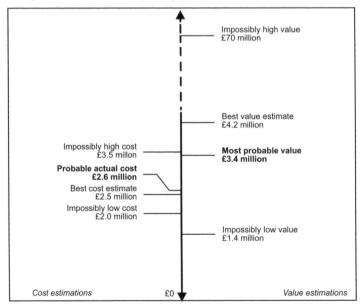

Figure 3.8   A cost–value estimate using the Monte Carlo box method

CONCLUSION

This chapter has described the main elements of the business case for a proposed project. Everything, from the business case report title downwards, must be led by the project objectives. Using the objective transform technique allows these objectives to be expressed as a series of recognition events and value flashpoints that provide an extremely valuable basis for planning and processing the project.

There can be as many different business cases made for the same project as there are different possible project strategies. So one business case must be analysed and presented for each of these strategies and each resulting business case report, together with all its associated calculations and charts, must be labelled with the appropriate case number to avoid costly errors when the preferred strategy is identified.

Lack of confidence in forecasts of benefits and costs can largely be overcome by using Monte Carlo analysis, the results of which are best presented in the format of a Monte Carlo box.

Once a business case has been approved, it becomes the basis for a project charter that will, when signed off, be the signal for actual work on the project to start.

REFERENCES AND FURTHER READING

Lock, D. (2003), Chapters 4 and 5 in *Project Management*, 8th edn, Aldershot: Gower.

Parkinson, C. Northcote (1958), *Parkinson's Law or the Pursuit of Progress*, London: John Murray.

Roetzheim, W.H. and Beasley, R.A. (1997), *Software Project Cost and Schedule Estimating: Best Practices*, Hemel Hempstead: Prentice-Hall.

4 *Planning*

Planning is the process of converting the business plan into a practical working document. This chapter considers the process from the point of view that failure is never an option, which means that the planning and subsequent control methods must be designed to ensure that all the intended project benefits are achieved in full and on time.

ATTRIBUTES OF AN IDEAL PLAN

A properly executed plan not only enables the coordination of people working on a project, but also the coordination of that project with other projects. The plan must be able to communicate what people have done, what they are doing now and what they will be expected to do. The plan is at the heart of the project; it is the most informative of all project documents and the common denominator for communication. However, planning is not always easy. Most projects are:

- complex
- subject to risk, uncertainty and change
- wanted as soon as possible.

The planner faces many problems. How can all the possible tasks that might arise be foreseen? How much detail should the plan contain? How should the plan be structured? How can interdependencies be managed effectively whilst avoiding gridlock? Project plans must be capable of meeting these challenges.

In the early years, between 1920 and 1950, planners had to be content with barcharts, now often called Gantt charts after Henry Gantt, the American industrial engineer who introduced them during the First World War. Since the 1950s planners have been able to express the complexity of projects far more effectively using critical path networks. Several variants of the critical path method were developed in America and Europe, but all allow the planner to record task interdependencies in a way that is not easily possible with Gantt charts. However, comprehending critical path networks requires some training; they are not a universally understood language and are therefore not suitable as universal tools of communication. For that purpose, Gantt charts still reign supreme.

Isochron simplifies the problem of multiple interdependencies by arranging project tasks in clusters of autonomous sets. Each set of tasks is bound internally by logical dependencies, but is loosely coupled externally with the other task sets. This minimizes dependencies between different paths in the network. Looking ahead to when the plan will be used for project control, the Isochron method recognizes that not every dependency shown on the plan will prove to be real when the time to start work arrives, and the project manager will often find (and, indeed, must strenuously seek) tasks that can be started with advantage before the network purports to show that they logically can. This approach (which will be explored and explained further in Chapter 8) can introduce an element of risk, but Isochron points out that the possibility of rework is often preferable to the certainty of delay.

Risk management (see Chapter 6) is a subject that has become better understood and more widely applied in recent years, and it is now accepted that planning should not be undertaken without consideration of project risks. A range of techniques has been developed to identify, assess and mitigate the effects of risk. In addition, procedures for controlling subsequent changes to the scope of a project are well known (see Chapter 9), although these are not so well reported in the literature. Whatever the procedures are for dealing with risk, uncertainty and change, the project manager must always be willing to question (and, if necessary, adapt or change) the solutions being followed. The planning method must be able to cope with all these possible sources of change. Thus it must be possible to change a project plan rapidly and easily in line with authorized project changes. The plan must also be updated whenever necessary to reflect progress. Plans drawn on paper or set up on wallcharts are not sufficiently flexible but, fortunately, plans processed by computer can be changed in a matter of minutes.

The best way to ensure that a project is completed on time is to manage the work effectively, using the methods described in Chapter 8. However, that can be done only if the plan provides a reliable 'road map' containing enough milestones (recognition events and value flashpoints) backcast from the end of the project to allow the project manager to question, measure, review and correct progress at relatively short intervals.

All of this raises the question of how much detail to include in the plan. Including a large number of trivial tasks serves only to complicate the plan unnecessarily. Having too few tasks, all with very long uninterrupted durations, is a step in the opposite direction of oversimplification. The experienced planner will know instinctively how much detail to include but a useful rule of thumb is to ensure that every task is interrupted (that is, divided into two or more tasks) at every point where it is expected to pass from the control of one manager, supervisor or technologist to another. Backcasting from the end goal (see the section 'Building backwards from the project benefits' later in this chapter) flows naturally from the use of recognition events and should be a constant guide for pruning out unnecessary detail and digression in the project plan.

As in so many other areas of management, Pareto's rule applies to project planning. Vilfredo Pareto (1848–1923) discovered during population census work that 80 per cent of personal wealth was distributed among only 20 per cent of the population. This has since become known as the 80–20 rule, in which 80 per cent represents the 'insignificant many', leaving 20 per cent as the 'significant few'. This rule is not confined to the distribution of wealth. It is universal in Nature. In work management, if you can focus your attention on the 20 per cent of the work that delivers 80 per cent of the desired results, you will increase your effectiveness fourfold. Taking this a step further, just 20 per cent of that 20 per cent will produce 80 per cent of the 80 per cent, and so on. The important point is that the same is true of the effort and cost invested in a project. Planning using the Isochron approach identifies and prioritizes the key 20 per cent of the project when it works backwards from the recognition events.

The plan must also be communicable. It must be possible to issue work-to lists, visually effective charts and other reports to managers and others after filtering and sorting the data so that managers get information only on tasks for which they are responsible. This is readily achieved by allocating appropriate departmental or resource codes to tasks in a computer system loaded with good project software.

SETTING THE TIME OBJECTIVES

Business plans should always be made before any technical solutions have been assumed, which means that the timescale for the whole project is almost always a given requirement. The outcome required by the business must be delivered, and the timing of the delivery costs and benefits is inevitably important. The first question for planning is not 'when?' but 'what?' and 'how?' and 'can we find a way to do it that makes it possible in the time allowed?'.

Identifying all the value flashpoints and recognition events is a matter of some special skill. In the absence of technical solutions, none of this initial planning can be performed using critical path networks or any other method that depends on detailed knowledge of all the tasks involved. So, even before the project manager has been appointed and the project authorized, the first stage of planning has to take place with very little detailed input. This is top-down rather than bottom-up planning, which means making a plan in coarse details from a project overview rather than attempting to build the plan up from all the detailed (as yet unknown) tasks.

The Isochron techniques involved in backcasting (abductive planning) are a very fast way of getting the planning started and 'right first time'. These techniques kill two birds with one stone by also delivering simultaneously a Pareto-based plan (see, again, the section 'Building backwards from the project benefits' later in this chapter). If the delivery dates of the recognition events and value flashpoints are treated as parameters that are given and key to the value of the project results, it is the question 'how?' (the nature of the approach) that has to be tackled in planning. If the project team were to be shackled to a single solution, where that solution has been given as if it were the objective, then there is a high risk that the deadline will become impossible. If the project end date is non-negotiable, then the project team *must* be given flexibility in choosing the solution. That is true 'agile' project management.

PENALTIES FOR MISSED DEADLINES

It is well known, empirically at least, that projects which run late also exceed their budgeted costs. Conversely, projects that are well planned and managed, and which are completed on or before their target finish dates, tend to run below budget. One important reason for this condition is that every project attracts an element of fixed costs – the costs of accommodating, servicing and managing the project. These fixed costs accumulate relentlessly for as long as people are working on the project, irrespective of progress made, and they will inevitably take the project into overspend if the work extends significantly beyond the date when everything should have been finished.

Engineering and other commercial projects can attract contractual penalties if they are delivered late, often calculated in direct proportion to the number of days or weeks by which the project overruns. Furthermore, when one project runs late, the organization often suffers knock-on effects, because resources and accommodation are tied up for longer than intended, delaying the start of projects and other work that should be following on.

For the kind of business change and IT projects with which this book is primarily concerned, late completion has other penalties. The business cases for such projects are built on the relationship between benefits and the times when those benefits should be realized. The net present value method of project evaluation described in Chapter 3 emphasized this relationship between time and benefits. Late completion of a business change project will delay the value flashpoints that should signal project success and, in a severe case, will result not merely in reduced benefits but in an actual loss to the organization. Such losses are often not simply monetary, but can also adversely affect staff morale and the company's reputation.

The British Library, the Holyrood Scottish parliament building and the air traffic control centre at Swanwick, Hampshire (Duffy, 2002) are just three examples picked at random from high-profile projects that finished well beyond public expectations of their costs and timescales. There are many (far too many) other equally well-known examples where expectations have been mis-set and mismanaged, often for political reasons, and where the projects have been delayed through poor preparation, planning oversights, uncontrolled changes, and contractual and financial difficulties.

BUILDING BACKWARDS FROM THE PROJECT BENEFITS

There are many high-profile projects where late completion would be disastrous and unthinkable, even though the projects are large, complex and fraught with risk. Think, for instance of a city's preparations for the Olympic Games, the Foreign and Commonwealth Office organizing a summit meeting of the G8 prime ministers, a royal occasion such as a coronation, a large public event like a pop music festival or the Chelsea Flower Show, or even an ambitious family holiday expedition. Although these are widely diverse examples, they all share one important common factor. Their finish dates are not negotiable. Failure is simply not an option (even if, sometimes, it comes perilously close). So how is it that these kinds of project do get finished on time, despite their size and complexity?

A large part of the answer lies in the determination of everyone concerned with the project to meet the end objectives. Planners' minds have to be directed not at determining how long these projects should take to complete, but instead at considering how they might, at the end of the project, have met their fixed 'wanted-by' dates; they must be directed not *towards* those dates, but must work everything *backwards* from them.

The obvious (but usually ignored) conclusion to draw from those public projects that traditionally are always ready on time is that the lessons learned should be applicable also to business change projects. If all the benefits set out in a business case are to be achieved in full and on time, then why not set their 'wanted-by' dates in stone and plan backwards from them? Isochron's objective transform technique does just that, using a particular human mental capability of memory and imagination that Tulving (1985) termed *chronesthesia*. In project management this means starting from the end value flashpoint and working backwards, first to identify and then to time all the intermediate value flashpoints and, back beyond those, the recognition events. This concept was introduced in Chapter 3, and is illustrated here in Figure 4.1.

The backcasting approach, together with other techniques described in this chapter, can be used not only at the start of a new project, but also to rescue an existing project that has run out of control. One example of this was a company with several product divisions that had booked a stand in a prestigious trade fair and was producing a number of products for display. These products included large steam and gas sterilizers, a de-Bakey heart-lung machine, electronic patient monitoring equipment for use in operating theatres and samples from a range of prefabricated operating theatre buildings. Six months remained to the exhibition and it was clear that no one knew the current state of progress or whether or not any or all of the exhibits would be ready on time. A 'crisis' project manager, directing a task force, was assigned to this problem. After discovering that the project was in a shambles, with no one having any idea of the current state of progress, let alone a practicable schedule, he decided to start from the only reliable constant, namely the opening day of the exhibition. His first question to a meeting of senior task force staff was:

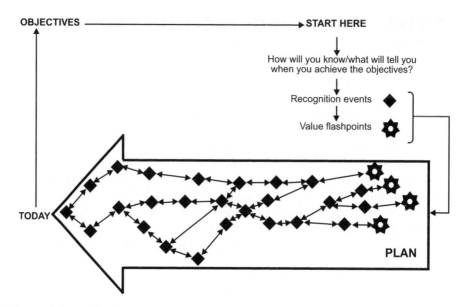

Figure 4.1   Recognition events, value flashpoints and project objectives

'What must we do immediately before the exhibition opens?' Answer (which had to be teased out): 'Final inspection and clean up of the stand.' 'What has to be done immediately before that?' produced more than one constructive answer, and the plan was worked backwards until the existing state of progress was reached to reveal a large number of (previously loose) ends. Using critical path analysis, the final schedule was then derived by working forwards, retracing all the paths and milestones that could only have been revealed by backcasting.

It is apparent from this example that planning needs imagination and, more than that, imagination informed by knowledge and experience. The people at this crisis meeting had to be coaxed and encouraged to use their collective minds to visualize the project at various stages in the future and work backwards from those. The best plans are always those that are reached by consensus, which has two important advantages:

1. Two minds being better than one, and brainstorming being better still, the collective brainpower will probably result in a plan based on the best technical process.
2. People who have helped to formulate the plan and who therefore agree with its implied method and milestones are more likely to commit themselves to its achievement.

Brainstorming with several minds is successful because, quite unlike a computer, the human brain is a *connection* engine. At a conservative estimate, the neuron network that powers an average brain has over *five trillion* connections. Thus the brain is extremely good at making connections – so good in fact that we do not hear all that 'intuition' tells us. Put two or more people together in a well-chaired meeting and the results will be vastly better than a plan produced by an individual working alone.

While brainstorming and the collective power of several minds can suggest a viable plan, critical path networks provide the notation that allows the plan to be expressed on paper and, eventually, in the computer.

So, for any new project built on the Isochron transform technique, we can imagine a newly appointed project manager assembling key members of the project team (business and IT) and asking them to think themselves into the future, when the project is complete. Then the manager asks them to cast their minds backwards from the value flashpoints, through the recognition events, until the project start is reached.

The product of the meeting will be a network sketch that contains all the significant known project tasks required to meet the needs and expectations of the sponsor and senior management – but no more! Once the duration of all those tasks has been estimated, the duration and critical path of the project can be calculated. This means making forward and backward passes through the network in a process called time analysis. The forward pass adds all the estimated task durations through each possible path in the network, from which the longest path indicates the earliest predictable start and finish times for every task and thus the minimum duration of the project. The backward pass mirrors this process by subtraction, to establish the latest permissible start and finish times for every task. For any task, the difference between these earliest and latest times is called the float (or slack), which is the amount of time by which one task can be delayed without delaying project completion. Tasks with zero float are critical tasks, and the path or paths that join them are also called critical.

Figure 4.2 summarizes the critical path method, using the example of an insurance company that has decided to move its customer services department to an offshore call centre. The network shown here has been kept simple for clarity, but it is sufficient to illustrate the basic steps of planning a project using the precedence system of critical path analysis. There are other methods of critical path analysis, but the precedence system is the only method supported by modern project management software. The precedence system and the other critical path methods are well described in the literature (Lock, 2003 and Gordon and Lockyer, 2005, being two of the many popular examples).

So far, so good. Working backwards from the value flashpoints should produce a practicable plan from which the project can be managed to achieve all the intended benefits at the times required by the business plan. All very straightforward – but with one enormous snag. When all the duration estimates have been applied, working backwards often finishes up not at the situation *today*, but *yesterday* (or even many days before yesterday). In other words, it seems that not enough time has been allowed to achieve the results because the critical path is longer than the time remaining from today to all the recognition events and value flashpoints.

Step 1: Identify the principal tasks and set them out in a logical sequence
Step 2: Estimate the duration of every task (weeks have been used in this example)

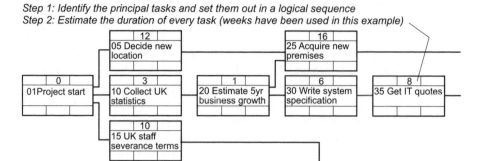

Step 3: Add the estimates along every path to find the earliest possible task starts and finishes

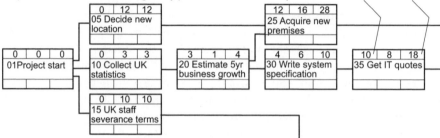

Step 4: Subtract the estimates backwards along every path to find the latest permissible times

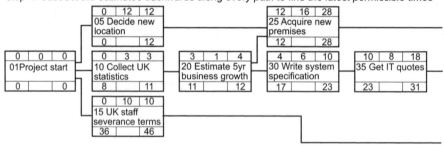

Step 5: Subtract the earliest times from the latest times to find total float and the critical path

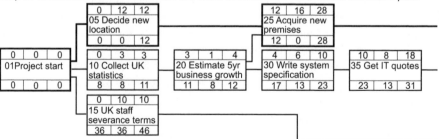

Figure 4.2   Five principal steps in conventional network analysis (precedence system)

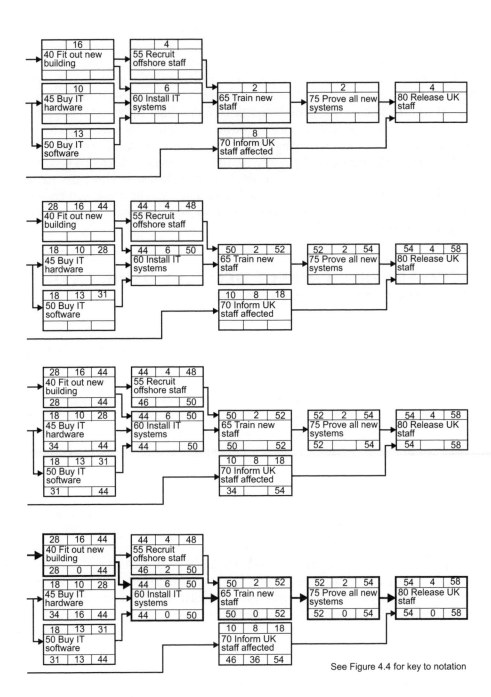

See Figure 4.4 for key to notation

However, this is not the time for despair. The simplest solution is to ask 'Is there another, smarter way to do this?' We regularly follow this practice in our private lives. When obstructed, we simply tackle the job in a different way – and often finish it sooner. There are at least two other well-known methods available to the project manager for accelerating project delivery. One of these is always known as crashing, which simply means throwing more resources at tasks on the critical path or finding alternative ways of accomplishing those tasks. Crashing can be very effective in projects such as construction, where the increased cost of the crashed tasks is more than balanced by the cost saving implicit in finishing the project on time. However, Isochron recommends avoiding that approach because, in a business change or IT project, it simply leads to more heads, more costs, more management overheads and more delay (see Chapter 6). The other well-known method is to take the plan by the scruff of its neck and re-examine it in a process known as fast-tracking.

ACCELERATING PROJECT DELIVERY USING FAST-TRACKING AND CONCURRENCY

Fast-tracking is a process well known to the managers of research and development projects where the time-to-market for a new product has to be as short as possible. If there are techniques that can reduce the total duration of such research and development projects, there is no reason why the same methods should not be used to accelerate business change projects and every reason why they should.

Traditionally, those who plan projects tend to string out the tasks end-to-end. Taken to its perfect limits, fast-tracking plans to do as many tasks as possible concurrently. Concurrency is part of Isochron's methodology. In fact, the company name is based on the term 'isochron', which means a line in space joining places of the same or equal time. The application of this concept to project planning can be illustrated by the very simple analogy in Figure 4.3.

Consider the process of taking shopping through a supermarket checkout. The upper diagram in Figure 4.3 equates to traditional, sequential project planning. Mr Jones joins the queue and, when he can, starts to transfer his goods from the shopping trolley on to the conveyor belt. Mr Jones waits until all the preceding shoppers have paid, loaded their goods into bags and departed. When Mr Jones's turn comes, he watches the checkout operator pass all his goods through the barcode reader. When, and only when he is asked to pay, Mr Jones reaches for his wallet, extracts a credit card, pays, puts the card and till receipts in his wallet, replaces the wallet in his pocket, loads his goods into carrier bags and leaves the checkout.

The next shopper in the queue is Mrs Smith. Her actions on reaching the checkout are depicted in the lower diagram of Figure 4.3. As soon as she can, Mrs Smith loads her goods on to the conveyor belt. She then finds her purse and estimates roughly how much her goods will cost. As soon as Mr Jones departs, Mrs Smith takes her trolley through the checkout to the far side of the till and starts

Case 1: Mr Jones, the serial planner

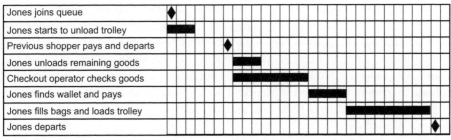

Case 2: Mrs Smith, the concurrent planner

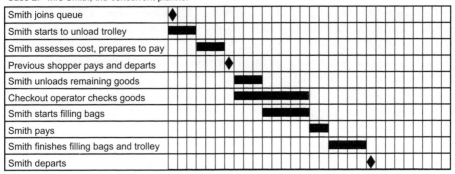

Figure 4.3   Serial and concurrent planning at a supermarket checkout

to prepare bags for packing. As the goods are checked through the barcode reader, she loads them into bags and puts them in her trolley. When the time comes to pay, Mrs Smith already has her purse ready and pays, either with her credit card and ready pen or PIN, or with the right amount of cash. After paying, she replaces the purse in her handbag and leaves. She has taken significantly less time than Mr Jones.

Mrs Smith has adopted the isochronal approach. Fixed in her mind is the outcome – to be walking away with the goods packed and paid for. She has planned her mini 'project' back from the point of leaving the checkout and is already thinking ahead to the chores to be done when she gets home (the outcomes of her next 'project'). She has, perhaps unconsciously, asked herself the following questions:

- What are the key things to be achieved in this checkout process?
- What tasks can be done simultaneously?
- What are the unavoidable dependencies?

Mrs Smith does not, of course, do this explicitly. Her outcome-based approach to planning this tiny project has become routine and instinctive.

Note that the resource levels are the same for both Mr Jones and Mrs Smith, comprising the shopper, the checkout operator, the shopping bags and the checkout equipment. Thus project compression and acceleration do not inevitably need duplication of resources. The values in this simple example may seem trivial, amounting to a few minutes of Mrs Smith's time saved and earlier clearance for subsequent shoppers. Similar planning and efficiencies can seem more important if you are delayed in a check-in or security clearance queue at an airport. In a project or programme of projects they can translate into savings of many months and millions of pounds.

So why do we plan projects any differently? The answer is not that we are, in some way, stupid. Rather it is that, although our *unconscious* thoughts are concurrent in the vast networks of our brain, our *conscious* attention is always sequential and single-channel. Pinch your arm and bite your lip at the same time and feel the sensation of pain flip between the two. Try as hard as you can, it is difficult to feel both pains with equal severity at the same time. 'Sensory gating deficit' prevents us from being overwhelmed with concurrent information from all our senses, memories and thoughts at the same time. It also makes us plan sequentially and causes us to add (Isochron finds) about one-third of redundant sequence and time into our project plans.

We can shed redundant sequence, shorten elapsed time, optimize concurrency of work streams and minimize interdependency by mechanically and systematically reorganizing the tasks in our project. Critical path analysis is a valuable tool for this process. The remainder of this chapter examines how the critical path method can be used to express accelerated plans.

USING CRITICAL PATH ANALYSIS TO EXPRESS ACCELERATED PLANS

With backcasting, skills management and fast-tracking available in the project planner's armoury, dramatic reductions can be made in the planned duration of most projects. Real project networks typically contain more tasks than can be shown with clarity on a book page (or on a computer screen for that matter) but, even in the absence of a large canvas, the principles can be demonstrated using just a tiny fragment of a network diagram, as shown in Figure 4.4.

Finding the minimum path using partial concurrency

The top diagram in Figure 4.4 shows two activities that lie on the critical path network of a first draft network for an imaginary project. An equivalent Gantt chart has been added to give a sense of timescale that networks cannot usually provide. This network plan has been drawn using the very common approach that shows rigid adherence to task interdependencies, with no attempt to accelerate project delivery by any of the methods described above. What this diagram shows is that

Serial (consecutive): 30 days' duration

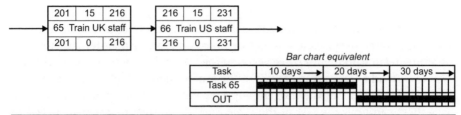

Partial concurrency: 20 days' duration

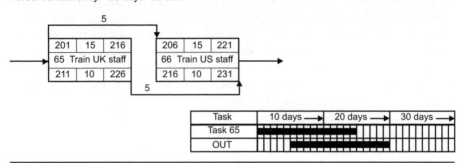

Total concurrency: 15 days' duration

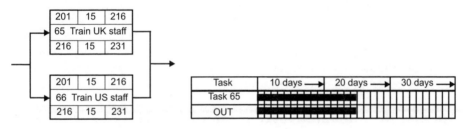

Key to notation

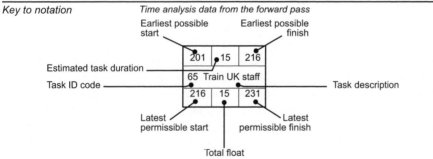

All time units on this page are in days, with 5 days in one week

Figure 4.4   Using precedence network notation to express concurrency

Task 65 must be completely finished before Task 66 can even start. The planner, in this case, has assumed that all training of UK staff must be finished before training in America can begin.

A common mistake in planning is to confuse resource constraints with work logic constraints. In this case it might be supposed that the planner has envisaged a training team working for three weeks in the UK, and then flying out to America over a weekend to repeat the process in the American branch of the company for a further three weeks. But why not employ a separate planning team in America and have them carry out the task at the same time? If we were to put that suggestion to the planner, he or she might argue that the second planning team would need a little training themselves, which could be provided by allowing the new team to work alongside the existing team for five days (one calendar week) to absorb the training method. This solution is assumed in the plan headed 'partial concurrency' in Figure 4.4. The simple finish–start constraint between the two training tasks has been replaced by a start-start precedence link which means that the American training can start five days (one week) after the start of training in the UK.

The five-day duration finish–finish link is necessary to complete the path for Task 65 and avoid leaving it with no successor tasks (in which case it would become something that planners call an end dangle). Dangling activities cause broken paths that prevent full time analysis. Devaux (1999) is particularly good at explaining the use of complex links in precedence diagrams.

This partial concurrency solution has reduced the total time needed for these two training tasks from 30 days to 20 days. These tasks were originally critical (with zero float) which means that, for the same project finish date, ten days' total float has been introduced into this path. Or, alternatively, the project could be finished ten days earlier (in which case the training tasks would again become critical).

Finding the minimum level of interdependency to achieve complete concurrency

If the project manager is asked to plan for the absolute minimum staff training time in both the UK and American companies, he or she must consider how to remove the interdependency between Tasks 65 and 66 altogether. This might be achieved by preparing two training teams in advance, so that both can be ready to start work on the same day and finish at the same time with the UK and American operations perfectly concurrent. Figure 4.4 shows that planning for total concurrency could reduce the total training time to just 15 days. So, by planning to eliminate the interdependency of these two critical tasks, the project close (and realization of benefits) has been advanced by three weeks.

A true case example of concurrent planning

The following is based on a true case, but dates and names have been changed to preserve anonymity.

A district council received a directive from the relevant ombudsman to implement a system that would make the allocation of local authority housing to the large number of applicants more impartial and objective. In July 2006 the council's small IT team planned the project and found that, if work were allowed to start in October, the new allocation system should be up and running 12 months later (in September 2007). However, ignoring this prediction, a prominent councillor (let's call him Councillor Sharp) not only announced the project in the local press, but also promised that the new system would be ready to accept applications by November 2006 and actually make the first allocations in January 2007.

The team were thereby presented with a shock requirement to complete their 12-month project in only half that time. An early project start was the first obvious step, but that would still only bring the system on line in July 2007. So, a fast-tracking approach was investigated, in which task concurrency could be maximized.

The team's first step was to list all the known tasks in the project plan and, temporarily ignoring resource constraints, challenge each task in turn to determine whether there was any sound reason why it should not be started immediately (or, at least, tomorrow). After challenging all the tasks in this way, a few were identified that could be indeed be started tomorrow. All the other tasks were dependent in some way on this first small group of tasks.

The team then re-examined all the remaining tasks to ask why each of them should not start immediately after completion of the first group. Again, some could, but the rest would be dependent on this second group. This process was repeated until the state was reached at which the last set of tasks could be started. It was found that this method caused the tasks to fall into a small number of parallel work streams, each largely independent of the others but with the tasks tightly linked by dependencies within their streams.

This revised plan initially suggested project completion by October 2006, but the addition of resource constraints indicated a practicable project completion date of January 2007. In the event the project ran just one month late and finished in February 2007, far in advance of the September completion planned without concurrent working.

CONCLUSION

Two themes run through this chapter. One is treating the time at which achievement of outcomes is required as non-negotiable. This is considered equal in importance with all the other qualities expected or the outcomes. The other theme is using recognition events and backcast planning to produce the most effective and practicable plan, together with alternative and contingency plans. The most effective plan can be made using the following steps:

1. Identify the recognition events from the sponsor and senior management.
2. Ensure that the recognition events and value flashpoints have dates attached.

3. Plan backwards from the value flashpoints to identify high-level key milestones.
4. Plan backwards from the key milestones to identify the technical and administrative processes.
5. Plan for maximum concurrency and minimum interdependency.
6. Express the plan in a critical path network using the precedence system.

REFERENCES AND FURTHER READING

Cross, M. (2002), 'Why Government IT Projects Go Wrong', *Computing*, 11 September, accessible at http://www.computing.co.uk/computing/features/2072199/why-government-projects-wrong.

Devaux, S.A. (1999), *Total Project Control: A Manager's Guide to Integrated Planning, Measuring and Tracking*, New York: Wiley.

Duffy, J. (2002), 'Cleared for a Very Late Take-off', *BBC News Online* at http://news.bbc.co.uk/1/hi/uk/1781780.stm.

Gordon, J. and Lockyer, K. (2005), *Project Management and Project Planning*, 7th edn, London: Financial Times/Prentice Hall.

Lock, D. (2003), *Project Management*, 8th edn, Aldershot: Gower.

Tulving, E. (1985), 'How Many Memory Systems Are There?', *American Psychologist*, 40, pp. 385–98.

5 *Project Authorization*

When the business case has been presented and the plans are made, the time has come to think about starting work. This is the point at which serious spending and commitment to the project will begin, so it is important to ensure that the project is started on the right foot and set on the correct course. It is the time when a final go or no-go decision must be made, when the business case must be given final consideration, so that money and other resources are not committed to a project that has no assured chance of success. The authorization process often consists of several approval steps, which will be outlined in this chapter. But, first, we start with a true story.

A CAUTIONARY TALE

A company commissioned a business case for the purchase of a complex and sophisticated software package. The business case document ran to about 30 pages, which included a cost estimate of £4.5 million against a predicted benefit value of £40 million. The business case was approved and signed off.

Some of the senior managers who had approved the business case were subsequently asked 'How confident are you that the costs will stay within £4.5 million and that the full £40 million will be achieved?'. The consensus was that there was only a 58 per cent chance that the total project costs could be held to £4.5 million. Further, it was considered that there was only a 27 per cent chance of achieving the predicted £40 million benefit. In fact, the general opinion was that the probable project value expectations lay closer to £11.6 million. Yet the managers making these fresh predictions were the same managers who had just considered, approved and signed off the business case.

This was not an isolated case. Political pressure can (and often does) force the approval of business cases where the ensuing project has no chance whatever of meeting cost, benefit and delivery expectations.

Isochron techniques were subsequently applied to the business case described here. That resulted in the following revised analysis:

1. Near-certain outcomes would be that the cost would be no more than £8.3 million against an achieved benefit of at least £30 million.
2. The proposed software package would account for only £6.8 million of the total expected £30 million benefit.
3. There was nothing to prevent work being started immediately on the project, independently of the software package, and realizing an eventual benefit to the company of £23.2 million.

In the event, the project was postponed for a very long time. That might suggest that the IT element, although not essential, was a catalyst without which management was not willing to change the business, no matter how compelling the cost–benefit analysis.

PROJECT JUSTIFICATION: REVIEWING THE BUSINESS CASE

The financial case

At first sight, a business case in which all the financial data point to a positive net present value and project success should mean that there is no reason why the project sponsor, or whoever else is responsible in the organization, should not immediately give the signal for work to start (and, of course, for spending to begin). However, too much emphasis can be placed on purely financial issues without considering the whole benefits package. Focusing only on the narrow financial implications of the project itself can lead to costly mistakes when secondary or incidental costs are not taken into account.

The business case, if it has been correctly prepared, should set out the benefits expected to accrue directly and indirectly from the project as value flashpoints, each with a date and value, and with the recognition events and causal milestones also listed. That process was described in Chapter 3. However, there is a complementary requirement, namely that there must be a process for tracking the recognition events and value flashpoints during and after the project to demonstrate clearly the success (or failure) in achieving each milestone. Will the company's accounting system be able to show the occurrence of each value flashpoint? If that is not going to be possible with the current proposals, the business plan and/or the accounting system must be put right before the project is allowed to proceed.

One company, for example, was considering a proposal for the complete re-engineering of the business. A project of that nature can wreck the business if the business plan is fundamentally in error. In this case, the proposal confidently predicted benefits that would be four times as great as the project costs. However, the proposal gave no corresponding indication at all of how performance towards achieving those benefits could be tracked. This meant that the company was being asked to undergo considerable upheaval and commit large amounts of money to a project in which the outcomes could neither be measured nor guaranteed.

Business plans are often unduly optimistic because they either fail to consider serious risks or understate the true costs. Described below are just three of the thousands of cases in which project authorization was contemplated against ill-conceived business plans that did not match total expected project costs with trackable benefits. These cases have been disguised to preserve their companies' anonymity and are presented in increasing sequence of project scale.

Case 1

A company occupied large offices in central London. At the time of the project, the managing director was ill and the financial director was on an extended overseas trip. Both these men had blocked any significant IT investment, and the small computing department relied on modem connections to external bureaux. The administrative director, deputizing for the managing director, found his way left clear to act on the computing manager's appeal and authorize the purchase and installation of an expensive server. The only costs built into the hastily prepared business case were the £50 000 quoted by the supplier for the IT hardware and software. The principal justification was that the system would immediately provide electronic office services that could eventually be developed for accounting systems and a management information system. Benefits forecast (without associated values or dates) were as follows:

- two fewer secretaries, owing to document standardization and re-use of stored texts
- elimination of external bureaux costs
- improved document presentation
- a management information system giving more accurate management accounting and project management data.

The facilities manager was instructed to find office accommodation and arrange installation, and to do it quickly before the two senior directors returned to their offices. Installation took only six weeks but then the problems surfaced. Project costs not included in the business case were as follows:

- office accommodation, which needed an architect to assist in gaining local planning approval for the building alterations
- hot water radiators removed and replaced by electric heaters (as no water was allowed in the computer room)
- partitions demolished and rebuilt with repositioned doors
- automatic fire detection and extinguishers (which worked well one exciting night)
- raised false floor in the computer room
- a 'clean' mains electricity supply, requiring expensive cabling and new switchgear

- signal cabling providing connection boxes to many offices in a large five-storey building
- underground cabling to annex offices (in pipes under a thickly concreted car park)
- additional printers
- redesign and printing of all the company's stationery
- training all secretaries to operate the cumbersome system
- a salary increase for one secretary, promoted to be the system manager
- very high maintenance costs on the computer after the expiration of the warranty
- £5000 added to the company's annual energy bills (with continuous day and night running)
- recruitment of two additional computing staff.

In addition, frequent computer downtime episodes left all the secretaries unable to access the system and no reduction was made in the total number of secretaries employed.

Case 2

A large financial institution investigated a proposed redesign and replacement of its core operating procedures. Considerable time and effort were spent preparing a business case document. All the financial tables were carefully laid out, showing a detailed budget and a forecast gross project cost of £6.4 million. The benefits to the company had been discussed at length among its senior managers and the project appeared to be well justified, but nowhere in the business case report was there any attempt to evaluate the benefits in relation to the £6.4 million cost. Nor was there any indication of how such benefits would be tracked and recognized when they were eventually either achieved or missed.

So, imagine being a member of the board of directors on being presented with this business case. You would be asked to sanction expenditure of £6.4 million on a project whose benefits might be classed as 'nice to have', but on which no value had been placed. Further, as this project proceeded, there would be no way of telling with certainty whether or not it had produced any benefit at all, because no method for measuring and tracking the benefits had been considered.

Preparation of this business case had already cost the company £500 000, yet its omissions meant that it did not provide a proper basis for project authorization. However, the business case was in fact authorized, which suggests that other (political) agendas were at play.

Case 3

A company prepared a very detailed description and cost estimate for the purchase and implementation of a £20 million IT system. However, in a business case report running to many pages, the forecast benefits were set out on just one line: a statement which claimed that the project would release 1000 staff from employment as a result of the project. No further explanation of the expected benefits was provided.

Any business plan that purports to make a significant reduction in staff numbers should always raise questions about how that reduction can be achieved in practice. How many of the people affected can be retrained or redirected to fill existing (genuine) vacancies? How many will actually go? Will they leave voluntarily or must compulsion be used? How will the trades unions react? What will be the costs of retraining, counselling and redundancy payments?

In this case, the new system did achieve the planned reduction in the total company workload as planned, but removing 1000 staff from the payroll proved impossible. To release that many people would have caused industrial strife, personal hardship and damage to the company's reputation. Only 100 staff actually left. The remaining 900 were eventually redeployed in jobs created for them elsewhere in the group. So the actual cost saving to set against the £20 million investment in IT was the payroll cost of 100 personnel. The salaries of the remaining 900 people had simply been transferred to different cost accounts.

PRACTICAL ISSUES

Apart from financial considerations, another serious issue before project authorization is whether or not the company has the will, determination and resources to carry the project through. How important is the project to the company and should authorization wait until one or more higher-priority projects have been finished? Some of these issues were discussed in Chapter 2. Moreover, should the business case be accepted in its entirety, or might it be necessary to split the proposals into a number of subprojects and reject or defer authorization of some of them?

Time required for project authorization

A project that does not start on time will probably not finish on time. For every day, week or month that the start is delayed, there can be a corresponding delay to project completion and the start of the benefits stream.

Preparation of a business case, even before project authorization is considered, can take months or even years. Some companies then spend more months, or even years, in considering the business case and deciding whether or not to authorize the project. Even when a tentative decision has been made to go ahead, even more weeks and months can be taken up in preparing the authorization document. Of course, adequate consideration must be given before a company commits itself to a substantial investment programme but, if competitors are not to seize the advantage, feet must not be dragged during the pre-project stages. In fact, there is every reason why simple planning and project management principles should be applied to the authorization process, so that (for example) drafts and redrafts of the proposal and eventual authorization documents are prepared and discussed without undue delay.

In industrial and commercial projects much of this preliminary discussion takes place during sales activity so that, when the external customer places an order for the project, the issue of an internal authorization document is routine and rapid. In the simplest case, the document is nothing more than a job order, of the kind that might be originated at the reception desk when we present our car for repair or service. Companies which regularly carry out industrial projects often issue project authorizations that, in hard copy form, cover no more that one side of an A4 sheet. For example, a London engineering company used the format shown in Figure 5.1 to authorize multi-million-pound mining projects as well as its own internal projects.

However, such brief authorization documents are usually backed up by a more detailed project specification. All that the authorization document does in many industrial projects is to allocate a project number, announce the budgets, set out a summary timescale, give details of the customer, name the project manager and leave communication of all the other complex data to other documents and meetings. Benefits are not listed in these simple authorization documents, even though the projects might cost many millions of pounds. That is because the estimated costs have already been balanced against assured revenue that is defined by the sold price or agreed scale of charges.

Business change and IT projects are an entirely different case. There is no external customer and the substantial investment required is not balanced by assured sales revenue. Instead, the principal determinant is the business case, preferably supported, in particular, by a value flashpoints register of the form discussed in Chapter 3 and illustrated in Figure 3.3. There might be considerable risk and scope for project failure. It follows that adequate time must be allowed for the process of reviewing the business case and preparing the authorization document. Will the project deliver the expected benefits? How shall we be able to track the benefits? What project management procedures will be appropriate? How is the project to be organized and staffed? It also follows that the authorization document is likely to be a fairly substantial document that will have great significance for the way in which the project is to be managed and evaluated.

PROJECT AUTHORIZATION

Client _____

Scope of work _____

_____

_____

_____

Source documents _____

_____

_____

Project number (to be entered by accounts department) ☐☐☐☐☐☐

Project title (for computer reports) [grid of boxes]

Project manager (name) _____ Staff number ☐☐☐☐

Project engineer (name) _____ Staff number ☐☐☐☐

Project start date (enter as 01-JAN-07) ☐☐-☐☐☐-☐☐

Target finish date (enter as 01-JAN-07) ☐☐-☐☐☐-☐☐

Contract type:

Reimbursable ☐   Lump sum ☐   Other (Specify) _____

Estimate of man-hours

Standard cost grade	1	2	3	4	5	6	7	8
Man-hour totals								

Notes:

....
Authorization (1)   Authorization (2)

Project manager		Marketing		Contracts dept.		Purchasing			
Project engr		Central registry		Cost/planning		Accounts dept			

Figure 5.1   Project authorization used by an engineering company

THE PROJECT INITIATION DOCUMENT (PID)

Once the decision has been made to proceed with a new project, the next step is to communicate its details to the project manager and all other key members of the organization. The principal and most usual method for performing that function is to issue a project authorization document. As explained in Chapter 3, project initiation for a business change or large IT project is a special case. It is common practice to issue a project charter or project initiation document (usually known as a PID).

Most or all of the project will be internal, with the project being conducted both by and for the company or group. Organization structures are discussed in Chapter 7 but the organigram shown in Figure 5.2 is fairly typical for a business change or IT project. The company is, in effect, both customer and contractor, with the contracting responsibility vested in the project manager. So the PID is a form of contract between the business and its own project manager. It is not a contract in the strict sense because it is not enforceable at law, but it nonetheless expects the project manager to comply with all the specified requirements, terms and conditions. The PID can therefore be regarded as a project contract.

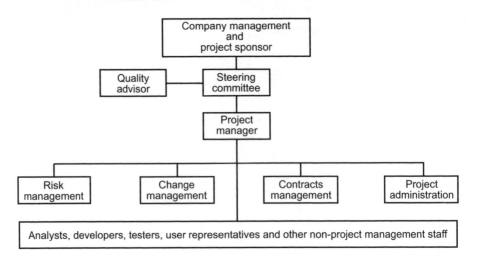

Figure 5.2   One form of project team for a business change project

Contents of a typical PID

The typical PID will, in most cases, include the key points of the business case on which the project is based. It is common to convert the original cost estimates into a new cost structure that comprises departmental and purchasing budgets plus suitable contingency funds. A vital element of the PID is the signature of the senior management member or project sponsor that actually permits expenditure to begin. The PID for a business change or IT project of any significant size can, unlike its counterpart in engineering and industrial projects, be a lengthy, even cumbersome, document. However, it does not need to be cumbersome. The key is to focus on the essential components and avoid the temptation to fatten the document by pasting in anything that looks vaguely related to the project. About ten pages should suffice. Rather than reproduce an example in its entirety, it is sufficient here to summarize the contents of a typical PID. Our example is taken from a real case and shown in Figure 5.3.

Project Initiation Document

Project name: Project number:

Contents

Authorization
        For the investment: (signed by a company director)
        For benefits realization: (signed by the project manager)
Document control
        Version control and issue date
        Distribution
Key project personnel
Purpose of this document
        Application
        Focus and closure
        Change and return on investment
        References and links
Contract summary
        Baseline state
        Details of subsequent changes
Objectives and scope
Deliverables (including the recognition events)
Benefits (including the value flashpoints)
Costs
Overall cost–benefit analysis
Sponsorship and stakeholders
Project team
Business team
Governance (project management methods)
Reporting requirements

Figure 5.3   Typical contents structure of a project initiation document (PID)

AUTHORIZATION IN THE ORGANIZATIONAL CONTEXT

In most organizations getting authorization for a project that contains any IT element has been developed into a multistage multilayered process. Projects that are exclusively about business tend to be authorized between the head of business and finance in the normal budgeting round.

The approval process is intended to ensure that budget is only authorized for projects that give good returns and align with company strategy. Small projects, however, are often signed off at head-of-business unit level, and escape under the radar of prioritization against other project investments across the company. Moreover, these projects are rarely checked for alignment with company strategy and objectives. Isochron has found that, more often than not, such small projects have zero or negative value, do not align with company objectives and sometimes outnumber key positive-return projects by 20 to 1. In addition, they use a disproportionate amount of IT and other specialist resources.

Larger projects will go through the head-of-business sign-off to a review by a project portfolio or investment committee. Before being presented to that committee they will have to meet certain standards of presentation so that they jump through predetermined hoops if they are to receive budget approval. The largest projects of all usually go straight to the project portfolio and investment committee. If they are signed off there, they must then also go through a board-level approval process before their budgets are confirmed. Thus the largest projects, which frequently include those promising the greatest returns for the company, often have the lowest chance of gaining budget approval.

We suggest that this common, but undesirable, state of affairs can be resolved by having a single portfolio into which all projects – business and IT and of all sizes – must be submitted if they are to get budgetary approval. The portfolio of projects should be systematically scored and prioritized against the organization's strategy and objectives, key performance indicators, critical success factors, balanced scorecard – whatever approach the organization uses (a process dealt with more fully in Chapter 2). An investment committee with board-level authority should meet at frequent intervals to review the priorities, commission or decommission projects and authorize their budgets.

The portfolio approach is currently fashionable, at least in theory. There are many tools on the market into which project business case and organization goal data can be placed and which redisplay the data for scoring and prioritization. The return on investment criterion is usually superficially dealt with. Powerful opposition to such an approach can come from senior people in an organization who want to get budget for their own local needs. They see a company-wide consistent prioritization and authorization process as an obstacle to their progress. By finding leaks in the process and by lobbying at board level they are usually able to push projects through that would not successfully get budget if objectively assessed against other investments.

Project start-up

Once a project has been authorized, the team must be mobilized and all its members made aware of their roles. This is best achieved by arranging a project start-up meeting (known in some circles as a kick-off meeting). This gives the project sponsor the opportunity of introducing the project manager to the remainder of the key team members. It also allows the sponsor or the project manager to outline the plan and purpose of the project. A well-conducted start-up meeting will end with all the participants being informed of the project purpose and description. Most important is that everyone should leave the meeting fired with enthusiasm and motivated to perform their roles so that all project tasks can be performed correctly and on time.

CONCLUSION

This chapter has described the crucial point in the project where the business case is reviewed to ensure that all the proposed project benefits will be both achievable and trackable. A positive decision must then result in the issue of a project initiation document, allocation of roles and the initial motivation of key staff at a start-up meeting.

6 *Risk*

A risk is a potential event that can threaten plans, expectations or even life itself. Devastating natural disasters, terrorist attacks and similar risks are often unpredictable and unavoidable, yet disaster contingency planning can often do much to mitigate their consequences and assist in recovery. However, many risks faced by project managers are neither unpredictable nor unavoidable. Once a project risk has been allowed to materialize it becomes an issue and it is too late to avoid the consequences. The motto 'Be prepared' should serve project managers as well as it does members of the Boy Scout movement.

INTRODUCTION TO RISK MANAGEMENT

Risk management is one of the most important, yet most difficult, areas of project management. Its importance stems not so much from the benefits that it might yield as from the penalties that it can prevent through foresight and planning to mitigate the worst effects of risk events.

In the late 1980s the UK suffered an unparalleled series of disasters, all of which cost many human lives. The following were among the most devastating of these tragic events:

- escalator fire at Kings Cross London underground station (1987)
- capsize of the Townsend Thoresen car ferry, *Spirit of Free Enterprise*, off Zeebrugge (1987)
- terrorist bombing of Pan Am Flight 103 over Lockerbie, Scotland (1988)
- destruction of the Piper Alpha North Sea oil platform (1988)
- many fans crushed to death at Hillsborough football stadium (1989).
  (*Source*: http://news.bbc.co.uk)

Partly as a result of learning from these events, Britain has developed world-leading techniques for disaster planning and risk management. Project managers, too, can learn from previous risk events in their own organizations and, from those experiences, develop risk management processes so that they can remain completely in control. The challenge lies in creating and operating robust risk management procedures that anticipate risk comprehensively, coupled with the authority to carry out avoidance and contingency actions in good time.

There is a clear distinction between risk and uncertainty. Risks generally include any specific event that can damage the outcome of a project, and that certainly gives rise to a great deal of uncertainty. But uncertainty about obtaining a particular benefit, or about the level of achievement, is not necessarily connected with risk events. To some extent uncertainty about achievements can be dealt with through Monte Carlo analysis (see Chapter 3) and this is the approach adopted by some project management software that purports to deal with risk. However, a different approach is needed to consider and 'manage' specific risk events.

Many aspects of project management rely on tackling problems in a logical sequence to arrive at a practicable solution. The acknowledged sequence for dealing with project risks is no exception. Although risk management is a continuous process that doesn't end until the project is successfully finished, it progresses initially through the following logical sequence:

1. Identify and list all possible risks.
2. Edit the list and record risks that deserve practical consideration in a risk register.
3. Analyse each risk to consider its potential threat to the project and express the results in a numerical score.
4. Rank all the risks in descending order of their scores, so that the greatest threats are at the top of the list.
5. Decide, well before each significant risk could materialize, what can be done to avoid or minimize its effects.

It is important to keep these steps separate because each performs a distinct function. This is one area where sequential, rather than concurrent, action is called for. Thus, for example, a meeting called to identify all the possible risks to a project should do just that, because to start thinking about contingency planning at that stage would divert time, effort and imagination.

IDENTIFYING RISKS

Above all, risk identification requires three things:

1. *Experience.* The organization and the project manager must be able to learn from the past and use that experience to visualize what might happen in the future.
2. *Foresight.* This is needed so that known factors can be applied to the forecast plans and expectations of the project.
3. *Imagination.* This is necessary to create possible scenarios that, although they might never have happened before, plausibly could happen during the lifetime of the project and are thus worth anticipation and contingency planning.

Most computers are sequential digital machines. Apart from inference engines and information storage and retrieval, and massive processors (such as those used to forecast weather), they use von Neumann architecture (Rojas and Hashagen, 2000). Outside the Internet and the World Wide Web, they are very poor at making connections. By contrast, human brains are connective engines. Everything that we learn and think in our lifetime is stored, retrieved and processed by the changing connectivity patterns in trillions of nerve connections in our brains. This enables each of us to envisage things that are not of the present, using processes that we sometimes call intuition and imagination (Tulving, 2002). Intuition and imagination are informed by a lifetime's experience stored in the same enormous volume of connective brain tissue. Every person (including anyone who is involved in any way with a project) carries this supremely capable organ around in his or her head. Thus it follows that if several brains with great experience of projects can be harnessed to think together collectively, an immensely powerful device is created that can comprehensively identify the risks in a project.

Methods for organizing collective brainpower

Given that two or more members of any project organization have enormous collective brainpower, it is appropriate here to consider methods for mobilizing that power for maximum benefit to the project. There are three dominant methods, namely meetings, brainstorming and structured walkthroughs. Any of these can be used to good effect in identifying potential risks. The three approaches share the same key requirements:

* Attendees should be selected for their knowledge and experience.
* Each meeting or session must be chaired professionally.
* Each meeting or session must be kept to its purpose so that, for example, a meeting to identify risks is not allowed to stray into the separate, subsequent process of contingency planning
* Meeting outcomes must be recorded, preferably straight into a risk register such as that illustrated in Figure 6.1 (see p.84).

Meetings

A well-chaired risk identification meeting will allow all attendees to:

* listen
* think
* exercise their knowledge, intuition and imagination
* make connections that identify risks
* speak
* be heard
* have their contributions recorded.

Unfortunately poorly chaired meetings are legion. In such meetings one or two attendees are allowed to dominate the proceedings. Mouths are engaged before brains. Some people might not be allowed to have their say, so that potentially valuable contributions are missed or overlooked. Even a productive session will lose its value if its results and benefits are lost through not being recorded.

Brainstorming

A well-facilitated brainstorming session will encourage free and untrammelled connection-making. It will enable the identification of risks, important and trivial, close and remote, and of high and miniscule probability. One of us recalls a brainstorming session in which an individual insisted that the risk of a meteor hitting the project team be considered. Although this might have been a significant risk for a nuclear power station, it was hardly worth listing for subsequent analysis and contingency planning for the business change project under discussion at the time. Nonetheless, the suggestion was recorded because a fundamental rule of brainstorming is that all suggestions be allowed and captured, with none ruled out no matter how unlikely it might appear. This leads to the point that a good deal of editing, structuring and value addition is needed after a typical brainstorming session.

Structured walkthroughs

Structured walkthroughs arguably offer the most valuable collective approach to risk identification. The method can be applied to any project episode, from the complete project outline considered at the early planning stages to a specific, complex part of the operation (such as IT roll-out plans in the middle project stages). Each episode can be slowly walked or talked through in the presence of all the people likely to be affected and who have the appropriate knowledge and experience. Everyone present should be encouraged to intervene whenever they identify a potential risk. It is crucial that such sessions should not be allowed to stray into the separate, subsequent process of contingency planning, because that would divert time and attention away from the primary purpose of identifying the risks.

RISKS IN ESTIMATING

Quite separately from the identification and management of risks to the project, the risk of under- or overachievement should be factored into the estimates of benefit values and of costs during the estimating process. When the Isochron techniques are used, in which benefits are identified by value flashpoints and the Monte Carlo box method is used as described in Chapter 3, then the risk management process is quite straightforward. Remember that, for each cost or benefit, three values emerge from this process, namely:

1. the highest possible value
2. the lowest possible value
3. the best estimate.

Having established these three values for a particular benefit or cost, the best estimate should be challenged. The process is reiterative and might start with the following questions:

- Given the past experience of the organization, how likely is it that the best estimate will be met?
- (*For a benefit value*) What is our organization's actual track record of realizing intended benefits?
- (*For a cost value*) What is our organization's actual track record of staying within this type of budget?

Now we can apply the answers to this history as a percentage factor to the best estimate. The challenge process then continues. For example:

- Do we know of any reason, or can we anticipate anything different in this particular project, that leads us to believe that the best estimate will not be met?

Then (if it is a benefit value):

- Does achieving this value flashpoint on our project depend on the outcomes of other projects or actions? If so, are we double-counting?

At each stage of the challenge process the best estimate should be factored appropriately. It is not uncommon to find that the risk-adjusted estimate of project benefits emerges as a small percentage of the original best estimate. Failure to take account of this risk effect when predicting benefits has caused non-achievement in many national and international projects.

An independent person should challenge the results of this appraisal again. Typically, this could be someone from the finance function or a business budget manager. They should ask the estimators questions such as:

- What makes you think that this or that event, which you have identified, will actually happen?
- Have you thought of *this*? Or *that*?
- Are you being unduly conservative or pessimistic?
- What facts make you think you are right?

Such dialogue helps to share ownership and understanding of the estimate between those who will track it and those responsible for achieving the budget. Initially it will secure their support in carrying the business case through the approval procedure, and it will also facilitate control of the active project.

CONTINGENCY PLANNING

If the purpose of risk management is to remain in control of the project at all times, it is essential to create plans for handling those risks that together present the greatest threat in terms of the perceived severity of their impact and the probability of their occurrence. The risk register illustrated in Figure 6.1 and discussed in the following section of this chapter is an essential administrative tool for this process.

Serious threats

Where a conscious effort has been made to learn from past incidents, successful issue management tactics and strategies can be embodied in standard contingency procedures. This has been the case in the UK, following the clutch of disasters in the late 1980s. Now, councils all over Britain maintain regional emergency planning units for dealing with risks ranging from nuclear and biological terrorism to aircraft crashes and major fires.

All organizations of significant size are required by their auditors to maintain disaster recovery plans for their business and their IT systems. For a particular project, contingency plans may already be in place but, inevitably, there will be some risks that are very possible, significant and unique to that project.

Each of the greatest risks to a project requires a contingency plan or, in other words, a 'What if?' solution. So, how can a contingency plan be created where none existed before? No prize for guessing here that the informed mind is yet again the most appropriate engine for the job. It can use imagination feeding off its lifetime of experience to make the new creative connections of a contingency plan. Once again, bringing several informed minds together in a meeting, brainstorming session or structured walkthrough increases the quality of the contingency planning.

Always remember that contingency planning is a distinct part of a sequence of steps. It is separate from the earlier risk identification sessions because those had a different purpose. Thus, because risk identification and contingency planning are different processes, their meetings cannot be combined and must be held on separate occasions.

Intermediate and minor threats

What about the risks that are perceived to pose a less serious threat – those which have a lower score for their combined impact and probability? These still require a measure of contingency planning but this should be scaled down to an appropriate level of effort.

For risks with the lowest scores it might simply be enough that the possibility has been considered to the extent that the project team has a feasible counter-tactic in mind: and in such cases documentation may not be required.

ESTABLISHING A RISK MANAGEMENT PROCESS

Risks can arise from the very beginning of a project, if not earlier. This means that risk management procedures must be in place before the project starts. It is good strategy to create and maintain a simple design for the risk management process. As with many other management procedures, complexity will inevitably tend to grow upon it – rather like the barnacles that grow on a ship and impede its progress. If the initial design is complex (and we have both seen some astonishingly complex designs) the procedure will eventually become unmanageable as further complexity develops. In the worst case, managing the management process itself will replace management of the risks. There is an understandable tendency for someone allocated the risk management role in a project to want to impress and perhaps justify his or her existence, and this may lead to the process being overengineered. The project manager should insist firmly on simplicity, focusing the risk manager's energy on the challenge of setting up a mechanism for rapid access to authority when contingency action is needed.

We have already discussed the initial processes for risk identification, and these should be institutionalized in the organization's procedures. However, there must also be a process that allows people to report and record potential risks that come to their minds at any stage in the project life cycle. Risk management systems that require people to fill in forms for this purpose are counterproductive and create unnecessary bureaucracy. The simpler, more preferable and most effective method is simply to advertise the risk manager's telephone number and e-mail address. Then, anyone who thinks of a previously unidentified risk at any time during the project needs only to be encouraged to e-mail, telephone or directly tell the risk manager.

Registration

Once a risk has been identified it must be recorded, usually in the form of a risk register (or risk log), an example of which is shown in Figure 6.1. A spreadsheet is ideal for this purpose. A risk register not only acts as a list, but also facilitates the initial assessment of each risk and records subsequent contingency plans and actions. It can also provide a check schedule for progressing subsequent reviews of each potential risk.

Assessment and scoring

Once a risk has been recorded, a subjective judgement must be made to assess the probability of its occurrence and the severity of the impact that it would have on the project if it should actually happen. The elements considered in risk assessment vary from one organization to another, but a fairly comprehensive set is shown in Figure 6.2. We find it sufficient to include the first three risk properties shown on our risk register in the figure, which are:

Risk ID	Date registered	Risk description and consequences	Probability P = 1 to 3	Impact (severity) S = 1 to 3	Proximity (time) T = 1 to 3	Ranking P x S x T	Mitigation or avoidance action	Owner of action	Date of last action/review

Figure 6.1   Part of a risk register (or risk log)

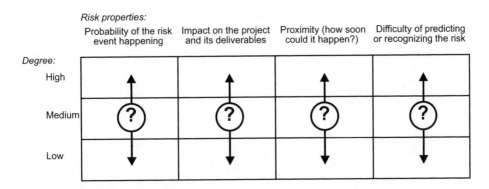

Figure 6.2   A risk classification system

- *Probability*. How likely is it that the risk will materialize?
- *Impact*. If the risk is allowed to develop and happen, how great might be the threat that it offers to project outcomes?
- *Proximity*. When could the perceived threat materialize?

A typical and practicable process uses a scoring system. Preferences vary, but Isochron uses a scale of 1 to 3 for each risk property, as indicated in Figure 6.1. Multiplying the three risk property scores gives each potential threat a factor that relates to its overall prominence and claim for attention. In our case, this score (or risk factor or risk rank number) can range from 1 to 27. Some systems use higher-ranging scores for each risk property (from 1 to 10, for example) but that results in some high numbers. A wide range of possible scores containing more than one significant digit might look impressive but, besides being unwieldy, implies an accuracy in the assessment process that is not justified because everything here is based on subjective judgement and best guesses.

The Isochron approach is to keep all the numbers simple. This is achieved simply by dividing the product of the individual scores by three. All the final scores (risk factors) then fall within a single-digit range of 1 to 9. Any decimals that arise during division are removed by rounding the scores to their nearest whole numbers (which can be done automatically by specifying zero decimal places when a program such as Microsoft Excel is used for the spreadsheet). This process results in a sensible range of risk factors of from 1 to 9.

Ranking (sorting)

When all the risk factors have been calculated it is essential that the risk register items are sorted and ranked according to their scores. Rows with the highest scores are placed first, with all other potential risks following in descending values of their scores.

Contingency planning and action can now more easily be focused on the risks with the highest scores. Isochron considers that scores of 9 and over are deserving of immediate attention, scores from 6 to 8 indicate the need for contingency planning, and scores of 5 and below should be monitored and reassessed periodically in case their levels increase. There is no point in dissipating scarce resources, cost and effort on risks that would have low impact or are unlikely to occur. If these low-score risks are subsequently considered to be more serious, they will earn higher scores and move up the table.

A cautionary tale

A risk register listing over 400 unranked and unsorted risks was presented to the project steering committee at one meeting after another, month after month, simply to provide evidence that risk management was happening and that the staff involved (note the plural) in risk management were busy and essential. The steering committee, although bemused and worried by the long list, felt totally unable to take any action on such a huge agenda of unstructured information. It reacted like the proverbial rabbit caught in a car's headlights: it froze in its tracks and took no avoiding action. Nevertheless, the risk management staff were still being paid every month for the perceived value of their efforts even though no action whatsoever was actually being taken to avoid the risks or to carry out any other contingency action. Each risk that did in fact materialize was simply added to an 'issue log', around which another industry of inaction was allowed to develop. That project was in deep and terminal trouble.

Of course that was an extreme case. But project control and survival often depends on taking simple and effective actions. In this case the remarkably simple action of sorting the risk register would have helped to save the project.

Action

The final important component in a risk management process is the action. There is no point in gathering and scoring risks and planning avoidance and contingency measures if action is not taken when it is needed. In any well-run business organization, action cannot be taken without authority. The authority needed to take many actions on risks often lies above the level of the risk manager, or even the project manager or programme director. Yet imminent risks demand immediate action. Action is needed before the risk develops or, at least, within the risk's materialization cycle time. Thus the risk management process must include a fast-path communication route to the highest authority. Care must be taken to pass only actions on high and imminent risks up this path to the highest authority.

Top people tend to be not always available, so one or more senior people must be designated so that there will always be someone at the top of the tree who can deal expeditiously with urgent demands for action. Care must be taken that only requests for action on high and imminent risks are escalated and allowed to travel up this lofty path. The default condition should be that the more junior person will take action, leaving the questions to be asked afterwards. It is often more appropriate to act first and apologise later rather than not act at all.

Another cautionary tale

A major consultancy firm was anxious to show that it was powerfully managing risk in a very large programme of projects. A complex scoring system had been developed, using impressive formulae and with possible scores ranging from 1 to 100. The risk register correctly contained columns like those shown in Figure 6.1. To show how effectively they were clearing up the risks, the consultancy team were keen to enter the sign-off date for each risk as soon as possible, but they chose to do this as soon as the person designated as being responsible (never one of the consultants) had been informed that the risk was 'Your problem'.

The risk register indicated an impressive risk clear-up rate. Yet risks were materializing all over the place. Simply telling someone that he or she has been made responsible for the risk is not the same as following up to ensure that steps have been taken to avoid danger or successfully implement the intended contingency action. That programme lapsed into deep trouble.

A risk must only be signed off (complete with a sign-off date) when the person who raised the risk agrees that it has been avoided or that contingency action has been completed successfully.

SPECIALIZED TECHNIQUES FOR CAUSE AND EFFECT ANALYSIS

Reliability engineers, quality engineers and health and safety practitioners use a range of tabular and graphical methods to help them examine the anatomy of risks. These methods were all originally developed for industrial use (such as in the automotive industry) but they can be adapted for use in risk assessment generally. Most of them require some training and can be time-consuming, even to the extent that a specialized consultancy and software market has grown around them.

There are several different methods to choose from, and each has many variations. They are interesting to us in one particular respect, which is that they are all backcasting processes that start by identifying a possible risk event (the *effect*) and then harness brainpower to work backwards and examine its possible *causes*. Contingency planning is generally not built into the methods, although preventive actions are implied because, once all the possible causes have been listed, avoidance measures become apparent. Among the many possible techniques, three are prominent. These are fault tree analysis, failure mode and effect analysis, and the Ishikawa fishbone diagram.

Fault tree analysis uses elements of Boolean algebraic logic. It takes the form of a tree diagram in which the risk event is placed at the top, with all possible branches ranged below. Paths divert through AND and OR gates. The chart can be quantified, with each possible cause being given a probability rating, so that these are processed up the tree to give a rating for the particular risk. A good example, which uses a car crash at a road junction as the risk event, can be seen at http://www.iee.org/Policy/Areas/Health/has26c.pdf.

Failure mode and effect analysis (FMEA) is a tabular method that lists risks events with their possible effects and causes. When scores are added, allowing risks to be ranked, the method becomes failure mode effect and criticality analysis (FMECA). The method bears some similarity to the risk register procedure, but is more analytical. An example is given in Figure 6.3.

Dr Kaoru Ishikawa (1915–1989) made many valuable contributions to quality management. His fishbone cause and effect diagram is particularly useful in recording the outcomes of risk analysis sessions. Unlike some other methods, its application is straightforward and obvious, so that no special training is necessary. An example of an Ishikawa fishbone diagram is given in Figure 6.4. For more on Professor Ishikawa, a good starting point is the excellent reference at http://quality.dlsu.edu.ph/chronicles/ishikawa.html.

Item		Failure mode	Cause of failure	Effect	Chance	Severity	Detection difficulty	Total ranking
Main building	1.1	Building collapses during installation of heavy machinery	Errors in floor loading calculations	Personal injuries Project delays Loss of reputation	2	9	5	90
	1.2	Building collapses during installation of heavy machinery	Floor slabs incorrectly poured	Personal injuries Project delays Loss of reputation	3	9	7	189
Security lighting	2.1	Some lights not operating	Lamps burning out	Reduced site security Risk of personal accident	1	4	1	4
	2.2	All lights fail to come on at correct times	Faulty switchgear	Reduced site security Risk of personal accident Risk of fire in switch room	2	6	1	12

Figure 6.3   Part of failure, mode, effect and criticality analysis (FMECA)

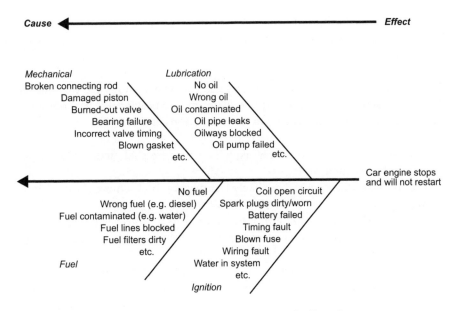

Cause ◄── Effect

Mechanical   Lubrication
Broken connecting rod   No oil
     Damaged piston   Wrong oil
        Burned-out valve   Oil contaminated
           Bearing failure   Oil pipe leaks
        Incorrect valve timing   Oilways blocked
              Blown gasket   Oil pump failed
                       etc.   etc.

                                                        Car engine stops
                                                        and will not restart

                 No fuel   Coil open circuit
       Wrong fuel (e.g. diesel)   Spark plugs dirty/worn
   Fuel contaminated (e.g. water)   Battery failed
        Fuel lines blocked   Timing fault
        Fuel filters dirty   Blown fuse
                 etc.   Wiring fault
     Fuel   Water in system
                                         etc.
                          Ignition

Figure 6.4   Part of an Ishikawa fishbone cause and effect diagram

Combining risk management and benefit realization tracking

Consider a project that has not only a risk management process in place and running as described in this chapter, but also uses the Isochron objective transform techniques of value flashpoints and benefit value estimating. In such a case it is both possible and desirable to combine these two processes to enhance the tracking of benefit value achievements.

Earned value, on the benefit side of the equation, is represented by:

1. achievement of the milestones and recognition events needed to bring about the value flashpoints
2. progress or timing of those events against the plan.

In order to achieve the benefit value, and to do so on time, it is necessary not only to make progress but also to manage risk to progress. The relationship between risks and benefits – or risks and value flashpoints and their value streams – is many-to-many. One value flashpoint may be threatened by more than one risk. These relationships can be recorded on a simple table in which the project risks are set out along the rows and the value flashpoints are assigned to the columns. Using this table it is possible to answer two key questions for the tracking of benefit realization tracking:

1. For this value flashpoint, what risks threaten the realization of its benefit?
2. For this risk, what value flashpoints (that is, the value in the project) does it jeopardize?

It is possible to progress further beyond the answers to these two questions. Given that each risk has a risk rating or score, and that each value flashpoint has an estimated value, the answers to four more questions can be found:

1. For this value flashpoint, how likely is it that we shall achieve the expected value of the benefit?
2. For this value flashpoint, how likely is it that we shall achieve the benefit when we expect it?
3. For this risk, at this moment, how much of the project value is threatened? Alternatively, what is it worth either to avoid this risk or to take a contingency action against it?
4. For this risk, at this moment, how much of the project benefit value is likely to be delayed (and, perhaps, for how long)? Alternatively, what impact is this risk likely to have on the project net present value and breakeven point?

These questions are likely to be central to the agenda of a project steering committee.

CONCLUSION

Good, practical, action- and outcome-focused risk management is vital to project control. Contingency planning and action should become a natural part of project life, enabling the non-negotiable recognition events and value flashpoints to be achieved by agile replanning and redirection. The project manager needs the freedom and flexibility to move from solutions that may turn out to be ineffective to other solutions that offer a better path to the outcome. The risk management process complements the change management process (see Chapter 9) to ensure that expectations are met regardless of events that threaten the project.

REFERENCES AND FURTHER READING

Association for Project Management (2004), *Project Risk Analysis and Management Guide*, High Wycombe: APM Group.

Bartlett, J. (2002), *Managing Risk for Projects and Programmes*, Hook (Surrey): Project Manager Today Publications.

Chapman, C.B. and Ward, S.A. (2002), *Project Risk Management: Processes, Techniques and Insights*, Chichester: Wiley.

Rojas, R. and Hashagen, U. (eds) (2000), *The First Computers: History and Architectures*, Boston, MA: MIT Press.

Sadgrove, K. (2005), *The Complete Guide to Business Risk Management*, 2nd edn, Aldershot: Gower.

Tulving, E. (2002), 'Chronesthesia: Conscious Awareness of Subjective Time', Chapter 20 in D.T. Stuss and R.T. Knight (eds), *Principles of Frontal Lobe Function*, Oxford: Oxford University Press.

Webb, A. (2003), *The Project Manager's Guide to Handling Risk*, Aldershot: Gower.

7 *Organizing the Project*

The most important resource in all projects is people. Project success depends on choosing the right people for the job, and then making sure that they are kept informed, well motivated and provided with all the tools and other resources that will enable them to complete their tasks. Part of those resources will be tangible things, such as office accommodation, furniture, tools, equipment, stationery, computer systems and other hardware. Some resources are not tangible, but are equally or even more important than those that can be seen and felt. Information is a vital resource from before a project starts until after it has finished. Information is useless without communication. Professor Hartman (2000) even went so far as to declare that '[poor] communication is the only cause of project failure'. So here we have a list of requisites that all projects need. This chapter examines not only how different project organization structures can influence people and affect communications between them, but also how the organization can either damage or enhance the management task.

ORGANIZATION STRUCTURES AND BEHAVIOURAL THEORY

Organization theory in businesses has occupied the minds of behavioural scientists for over a century, but formal organization structures can be traced back to the beginnings of history, particularly in churches and armies. The subject is complex. Organizational behaviour will always provoke discussion and debate among managers. Huczyinski and Buchanan's classic book on organizational behaviour is a huge tome that runs to over 900 large-format pages, yet it claims to be only an 'introductory text' (Huczyinski and Buchanan, 2001). Project organization theory is well supported in the general literature – for example in Meredith and Mantel (2003).

Choosing the organization structure that best suits a particular business of project is not always cut and dried, and in some circumstances competing companies might fare equally well even though their organizational structures differ considerably. In business change and IT projects we are fortunate that a clear solution presents itself, with no feasible alternative. By describing some of the organizational forms that can be used in projects, we shall be able to show why the task force is the only sensible option for a business that wishes to accelerate its change project to a successful conclusion in the shortest possible time and with the least possible amount of conflict and other people problems.

Project organizations vary enormously from one company to another, but almost any organization can be analysed and categorized as being one of the following:

- a matrix
- a team
- a hybrid, in which elements of both team and matrix are mixed.

To support our argument in favour of the task force (a variation of a team structure), we need consider only the first two of the options listed above. For simplicity, we shall refer to company organizations throughout, but the same arguments apply exactly to projects carried out by other bodies such as government departments and not-for-profit undertakings.

MATRIX STRUCTURES

The common theme in all matrix structures is that authority and power between the project manager and functional managers in the company are, to a greater of lesser degree, shared. The basic idea is presented in Figures 7.1 and 7.2. Not long ago, management scientists raved about this kind of organization and it was thought to be the best invention since the safety pin, the mousetrap or sliced bread. Now, wiser and more experienced opinions prevail, and we know that the matrix may not always be the appropriate choice.

The organigram in Figure 7.1 shows the kind of matrix organization that is often adopted when a company has no previous experience of projects but wishes to undertake a single project, either for an external customer or to manage an internal change. The existing organization is left untouched, but a 'project manager' is appointed to plan and coordinate the project work. For that reason, this pattern is often described as a coordination matrix. An alternative name is 'overlay matrix', because the project organization is overlaid on the existing structure. However, the 'project manager' here has no real authority and is little more than a coordinator. When a company makes the mistake of choosing a matrix organization for an important business change project, it will become obvious that the project manager does not have sufficient power and authority to carry the day. Communication (such as meetings) between staff working on the project quickly becomes a heavy overhead. Other disadvantages of the matrix organization are summarized in the section 'The case against the matrix', later in this chapter.

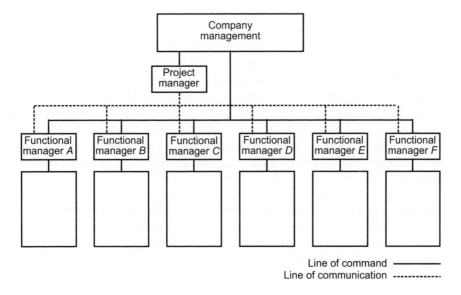

Figure 7.1   A coordination or overlay matrix organization for a single project

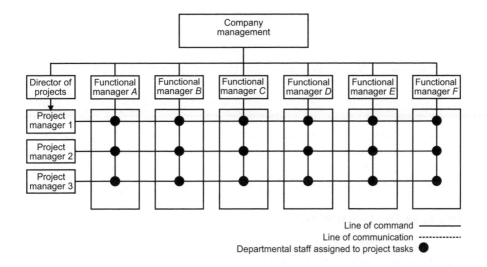

Figure 7.2   A matrix organization for more than one project

The matrix structure shown in Figure 7.2 is used when the company is simultaneously carrying out more than one project. It is simply a coordination matrix that has been logically extended to accommodate more than one project manager.

Different strengths of the matrix

Organigrams do not always convey all the subtle nuances of an organization in practice, and they are not particularly successful at showing how power is shared between the project manager and the functional managers in a matrix. To resolve this problem we supplement the organigram by giving the matrix a title that remedies this deficiency. The following summary lists the more common matrix organizations in ascending order of power owned by the project manager. A matrix where the project manager has little power is called a weak matrix, and a strong matrix indicates that the project manager has more power than the functional managers.

- *Coordination matrix.* The project manager has absolutely no authority, but can only coordinate and advise. The project manager must use persuasion or apply to higher management to implement any action that he or she might require when cooperation from functional managers is not forthcoming.
- *Balanced matrix.* Power is shared equally between the project manager and the functional managers. The idea is that the project manager directs work progress, whilst the functional managers allocate the most appropriate staff and monitor quality. Conflict often results, particularly when more than one project manager clamours for scarce resources or when a project manager disagrees with a design solution or problem approach instituted by a functional manager.
- *Strong matrix.* Higher management give special support to the project manager and make it known through the company communication system that, should conflict arise, the project manager has the final decision and therefore has more power than the functional managers.
- *Secondment matrix.* A very strong form in which the project manager is given far more power than the functional managers to the extent that he or she may nominate people from the functional departments and have those people seconded to the project for as long as the project manager wishes. This is very similar to the task force concept described later in this chapter and is the only form of matrix that should ever be considered for a business change project.

The case for the matrix

The matrix organization is attractive to companies that regularly handle a succession of projects, particularly where many of those projects take place simultaneously. It requires least thought and effort to implement, and makes little apparent impact on the existing organization structure. The functional organization remains stable as projects come and go, and the functional managers and their subordinates build up technical experience. It is claimed, therefore, that the balanced matrix is conducive to high technical quality. People working in a matrix feel that they have stable employment, which is not dependent on a single project. They might even find themselves working on two or more projects simultaneously or being switched between projects. A person working within a functional department can see a career path ahead, which includes promotion within the functional department even unto the glorious heights of departmental manager.

Where several projects compete for scarce common resources, or perhaps for the one person in the company who is blessed with a special skill, the matrix arrangement provides the flexibility necessary to deploy resources most effectively and divert them, when required, to projects with the greatest need. So, a matrix organization is inherently more flexible and efficient in the allocation of scarce resources across a number of simultaneous projects.

The case against the matrix

A matrix organization breaks a fundamental rule of management by violating the principle of unity of command. In other words, a person working in some forms of the matrix can find him- or herself working for two different masters (the project manager and the specialist function or line manager). Where the two managers agree, there is no problem. However, when conflicting instructions are given, mayhem results.

For example, the line manager responsible for the development, pay and rations of a member of staff might want to give that individual (George) work other than that demanded by the project manager. The line manager might even decide that George should be allowed time off for training or insist that his annual holiday entitlement must take priority over project work. The project manager, on the other hand, is responsible for the successful completion of the project and so has different priorities. He or she might want to insist instead that George must work exceptionally long hours, with no question of interruption for training or annual holiday until the project task is done.

One of us (DL) once worked in a matrix where the project manager was divorced from the functional manager's sister. That employment lasted for six months (three months finding out and three more looking for another job).

A matrix organization is not best suited to communication between project participants, who may be scattered among different offices and even in different buildings or locations. Yet those conditions are usual in large projects and programmes.

Maintaining confidentiality of proprietary information can also be very difficult in a matrix, because its members are constantly mingling with others who are not working on the same project. That can prove particularly serious in a business change project because leaks and gossip are apt to generate rumour, myths, disquiet, apprehension and even unnecessary industrial action amongst the company's general workforce.

Achieving a team spirit in most matrix organizations is a difficult task for the project manager, because no real team actually exists – there is simply a workforce allocated to the project by the functional managers. And that workforce can be constantly changing at the whim of the functional managers who allocate people to tasks.

However, the adoption of a secondment matrix will negate many of these disadvantages.

PROJECT TEAM STRUCTURES

A project team structure is, at first glance, far simpler than any form of the matrix although it requires more thought, change and authority to implement. A project manager is appointed and put in complete command of all who work full-time on the project. Functional managers are not simply given less power than the project manager, but they actually report in direct line of command to him or her. The organigram in Figure 7.3 shows just such a team.

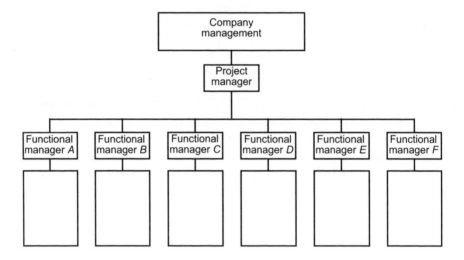

Figure 7.3   A pure project team organization

Team complexities

In practice, of course, there might be complications that prevent the organization from being a simple team. For instance, the project manager will not usually have complete authority over external agencies and suppliers. So, it is rare for a project manager, even in a team organization, to have complete autonomy over everyone working on the project. However, that difficulty can be overcome to some extent if suitable contracts are agreed with external agencies and suppliers.

Teams within teams

Teams exist within teams. We may belong to a project team, which in turn belongs within a programme team, which in turn belongs within the company 'team' and so on. The following case will help to explain what a team is, for project purposes. It is set in a supermarket with 24 checkouts. At each checkout there is a checkout operator and a queue of customers.

Consider what should happen at each of the 24 checkouts. For perfect operation, the following conditions must exist:

- All the goods in the current customer's basket are correctly barcoded.
- The customer has enough money to pay for the goods.
- None of the goods is damaged.
- There is no problem with the checkout technology.

Under these perfect conditions, the customer and the checkout operator form a classical team (in this case, of two people) dedicated to the task of getting the goods checked out and paid for. This team has all the equipment, goods and skills needed to reach the task (or project) objective.

Now what happens if one of the items is not barcoded at checkout number 1? The checkout operator stops, hits an alarm button and then waits. A bell and flashing light operate at the checkout to alert and summon the supervisor. But the supervisor has to deal with all the other 23 checkouts. All the customers in the queue at checkout 1 must wait until the supervisor becomes free. At that point we suddenly have one team of over 50 people, comprising all 24 checkout operators, their customers and the supervisor.

In other words, a logical team is glued together by (1) having a common objective and (2) having all the resources and capability needed to attain that objective. For a team to operate properly and efficiently it must neither have multiple alternative objectives nor be expected to compete for resources and capability. Otherwise the leadership, authority and even the competitive power of a project manager are all that stands between the team and chaos. No wonder chaos is so common in business and IT change projects.

The task force

A task force is a special case of team organization. It possesses all the advantages (and disadvantages) of the team but is even more project-focused. It implies a team that is set aside from the main company organization, perhaps even being located in a specially designated office and having great power to make decisions that can even affect parts of the organization that are not directly engaged on the project – in fact, all the prerequisites for a business change project.

An extreme case is the 'virtual company'. Here a unit is established that consists of participants from all the suppliers. This unit acts for the duration of the contract as if it were a separate company, an arrangement that has sometimes been used (for example, in the utility and energy sectors) to accomplish projects where the time and cost constraints are too tight for normal approaches.

The case for the team

The case for the team, especially from the project manager's point of view, is at first sight compelling. There is unity of command, and the opportunity for conflict is minimized. If people actually belong to a real team (as opposed to the virtual team in a matrix) the project manager's task in generating a team spirit is far easier. People in a team are better motivated and can easily identify with the project and its outcomes. Communication between team members is relatively easy. Confidentiality of sensitive information and documents is made easier, because discussion takes place only between team members who can, in the best arrangement, be located together in one office or building. In fact, how can one generate team spirit if no team actually exists?

The case against the team

It is easy to motivate a team during the early and middle stages of a project. People naturally become enthusiastic, particularly if the project has a high profile or exercises creative skills. But, as the project nears its end, people start to wonder where their next work will come from. Is there another project waiting in the wings or shall we receive only congratulations on a job well done, and will the end of the project coincide with the end of our employment? Consideration should be given to the possibility of keeping a successful team together and moving it from project to project, although this can cause problems in respect of motivation and personal development.

Self-contained, dedicated project teams can be inefficient and inflexible in the use of scarce resources. Suppose, for example, that a buyer is appointed to the project team. If that buyer were working in a purchasing department, his or her time would be spread over many different projects. But place that buyer in a project team and there might be many hours, or even days, when he or she can find nothing useful to do. To avoid this difficulty it is essential that team members are, as far as possible, multiskilled. Otherwise a company that regularly uses several project teams might find that it has to recruit additional staff to counteract the inflexibility of redeployment that the team structure tends to create.

CREATING A TASK FORCE FOR BUSINESS CHANGE

When any project gets into management difficulties and the project doctor is called in, one of the first things that must be looked at is the project organization. And the best form of organization for rescuing a drowning project is a rapidly and specially convened task force. So, if a task force is the best organizational form for accelerating a project to its successful completion, why not organize a business change or IT project as a task force from the start, before the project is allowed to falter and fail?

Figure 7.4 illustrates the formation of a task force from and within an existing company organization structure. The upper half of the illustration shows a task force embedded in its parent company, whilst the lower half of the figure has dissected the task force elements from the whole to provide a clearer picture of its structure.

The first essential is to appoint the project manager. He or she will probably be an existing manager from within the organization, but it might be necessary to buy in a professional. The project manager should have at least a basic appreciation of project management methods but, above all, must have drive, determination, a motivating personality and the ability to carry the project through despite all its actual and potential difficulties.

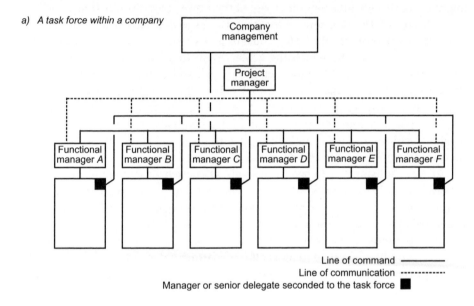

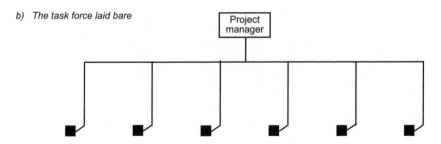

Figure 7.4   A project task force organization suitable for a business change or IT project

Establishing the task force

Staffing

Before considering the constituents and arrangement of the task force, consider first what its attributes must be. For a business change project, the first requirement is an in-depth knowledge of the existing business, both internally and externally. If there is going to be change, the task force must first know what is going to be changed! That usually means an in-depth study of existing practices, procedures, jobs and departments. The best equipped task force will contain representatives from all the key departments, who are sufficiently senior to understand how potential changes might act to the advantage or otherwise of their own specialist functions.

Collectively, the task force must have the expertise needed to appreciate all elements of the business plan. They must be able to focus on the expected benefits and know the means by which the achievement (or non-achievement) of those benefits can be recognized. When actions are demanded, the task force must have the authority to carry them out without delay, which means without having to refer unnecessarily up the management chain of command for approval. This all suggests that task force members should be individuals who are accustomed to making decisions and who can be trusted with delegated authority. A task force is no place for wimps, cissies and amateurs.

So the establishment of a task force requires that each key functional department manager whose work comes within the orbit of the project should allow a senior member of his or her department to join the project team. Further, the person appointed in each case must not only represent the needs of the particular specialist function, but must also be empowered with delegated authority to make decisions and act without referral to seniors. If a departmental manager does not have sufficient confidence in the delegate that he or she has chosen, that delegate must either be replaced with a person who does command the necessary confidence or the departmental manager must appoint him or herself to the task force for the duration of the project.

Should it become necessary to augment or support the task force by engaging contract staff, those staff must be expert in the required specialist fields. This aspect is discussed further in Chapter 8.

Location

The task force should be given a base location, where working papers can be locked up overnight and where work, planning, informal discussions and formal meetings can all take place in a secure environment. The place chosen must have access to the company's existing IT systems and have good external telecommunications. Most important of all, establishing a location where all members of the task force can work together, unhindered and uninterrupted by their parent departments means that internal project communication will be as good as one could ever get.

An essential part of the accommodation is a task force common room – a meeting place that is sometimes called a 'war room'. This is project territory. Walls and tables can be covered with working documents and plans, and these can be left out all the time because the room is dedicated to the project. Prominent among the wallcharts must be a map of the project's recognition events and value flashpoints, so that every team member is kept constantly aware of the project's intended outcomes and daily progress can be tracked against the expected benefits.

ORGANIZATION DIFFICULTIES AND SOLUTIONS FOR LARGER PROJECTS

So far in this chapter, all the discussion has assumed that the project will be conducted within a single company, requiring a task force numbering just a few highly capable individuals, working directly for one project manager. However, this solution will simply not work for larger projects, especially where the business change or IT is going to affect several companies within a group. The only way of ensuring that the particular needs of each business within the group are considered and catered for is to enlarge the task force considerably to accommodate full- or part-time delegates from all the companies involved. Larger organizations have more complex communication requirements, and more attention must be given also to the way in which the project manager's authority is delegated through functional and other managers.

A programme director and programme manager should be appointed to manage the complexity of interdependencies and communications across the multiple business- and technology-changing projects that are likely to be involved in the change programme. The project managers of the individual projects will be directly responsible to the programme manager. A programme support office, staffed with perhaps a half-dozen individuals, will be needed to support the programme manager and the project managers with cross-programme planning, risk management, contract management, change management, benefit realization management, cost control and quality assurance services.

Complexity in communication

Isochron claims that the contribution to project work made by each additional team member, no matter how highly skilled, reduces progressively as the team becomes larger owing to the increased complexity of internal team communications. This is illustrated by the graph in Figure 7.5, which shows that, by the time the size of a single group reaches 30 people, each additional person, surprisingly, contributes nothing further to the project. This suggests strongly that large functional groups should be divided into smaller units. A work breakdown arrangement can suggest how this might be arranged, perhaps by breaking to the project organization down into groups that match one or two work packages.

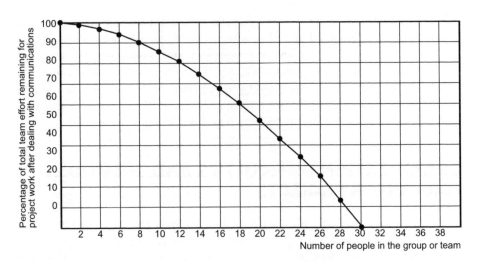

Figure 7.5   Relationship between team size and team work output (empirical)

A manager's span of control

Ever since the work of Graicunas (1933) it has been recognized that there is a practical limit to any manager's span of control – in other words, the number of people reporting directly to the manager should not be so great that the manager is unable to give sufficient time and attention to the work and problems of those reporting directly to him or her. People disagree on how great this limiting number should be, but the 'rule of five' or 'rule of seven' are often used as guidelines in organization design.

It is likely and desirable that line managers will want to have a one-to-one meeting for development purposes with each of their direct subordinates at least once every two weeks. This allows each manager to ensure that the roles are being delegated successfully and helps to promote good understanding between managers and their subordinates. Assuming that each such meeting would last for an average of about one hour, a line manager with seven direct subordinates would be devoting time to this essential management activity that equates in total to about one in every ten working days.

Divisional or federal structures

Difficulties of scale are discussed in greater detail in Harrison and Lock (2004), and one solution that they propose is the divisional or federal organization (Figure 7.6). In this case, the main project is split into a number of subprojects, each of which is placed under the command of its own manager. The advantages of team or task force organization are retained because all project managers report directly to the programme manager.

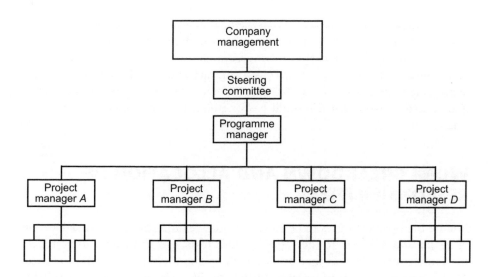

Figure 7.6   A divisional project team for a larger project

A divisional or federal structure can simplify the detailed planning and scheduling problem for a large project, because a summary plan, backcast from the recognition events and value flashpoints, is all that the programme manager needs to produce. Each project manager can then be asked to produce a detailed plan for the tasks under his or her command.

Delegating the PID contract implications

Although the project or programme manager will always remain responsible for meeting the contract details set out in the PID, in a large organization some of the commitments must be delegated to more than one project manager. Thus, between each project or functional manager in the team and the programme manager there exist a number of agreements or informal contracts on the work to be done for the project. The total effect of all these informal contracts must be equal to the requirements of the total project contract or PID. This dispersal of contractual responsibilities through an organization is sometimes known as a contractor–consignee arrangement and it has some similarities with the way in which an organization's overall objectives are diluted and dispersed from the CEO downwards in a management by objectives process. For the large project organization, each diluted portion of the PID should contain at least one recognition event.

Increased role for the steering committee

The larger and more complex the organization becomes, the easier it is for the project manager to lose sight of the overall project objectives (as outlined in the business plan). For this reason the steering committee has a bigger and more important role to play in larger projects, being responsible to the project sponsor to ensure that the project stays on track to achieving all its intended outcomes.

Isochron suggests that the steering committee will be able to control the programme well if it treats the PID as a contract and imposes a formal change management procedure to control all proposed changes to the contract terms that exceed a significant threshold (see the discussion of change management Chapter 9).

WORK BREAKDOWN AND ALLOCATION OF RESPONSIBILITIES

Among the practical issues to be solved at project authorization is the allocation of people and resources to the various project tasks. The first step is to nominate the project manager, and then to decide upon the project organization needed. Of the various project organization structures discussed above the most suitable organization for a 'one-off' business change or IT project will most likely be some form of team or task force. The project organigram should be annexed to the PID if possible or, otherwise, it must be given at least the same distribution as the PID.

A tool that is commonly used throughout all kinds of projects to choose and announce the allocation of project duties to people is the responsibility matrix. An example is shown in Figure 7.7. The roles used in this case broadly correspond to the organization depicted in Figure 5.2 (p.72).

Task	Responsibility	Steering committee	Sponsor	Quality assurance	Project manager	Risk manager	Change coordinator	Project administrator	Purchasing manager
Project steering and direction	✓	✓			✓				
Project management methodology	✓	✓			✓				
Meetings management			✓		✓				
Planning					✓				
Resource allocation					✓				
Estimating					✓				
Project initiation					✓				
Risk management				✓	✓	✓			
Benefits realization			✓	✓	✓				
Change control					✓		✓		
Configuration management					✓			✓	
Quality advice				✓					
Quality and testing				✓	✓				
Suppliers/contracts									✓

Figure 7.7   A linear responsibility matrix – for matching tasks to organizational roles

Strictly speaking, a responsibility matrix should not (as we have shown) allow for more than one person to be responsible for the same task. Making two or more people responsible for the same task is introducing a serious risk that none of the people listed will take any action, each assuming that the others are performing the task. So most responsibility matrices use two different symbols, to represent two kinds of responsibility – primary and secondary. The person nominated as being primarily responsible has the burden of ensuring that the task is performed, whereas the person with secondary responsibility must be involved through consultation.

CONCLUSION

Organization theory is complex, and people might disagree about which organization is best for particular kinds of projects. However, we have shown in this chapter that, for business change and IT projects, the best solution is to establish a project task force, staffed only with experts, who are empowered to make decisions. Further, the task force must be located in a secure environment where they can work without interruption, and be grouped together to allow the best possible communication within the project team. If the project is so large that the task force numbers would approach or even exceed 30, there is a strong case for creating a programme with a divisional or federal structure containing several projects. In larger projects the need for a steering committee is more pronounced and its role becomes more important.

REFERENCES AND FURTHER READING

Belbin, R. M. (2003), *Management Teams: Why They Succeed or Fail*, 2nd edn, Oxford: Butterworth-Heinemann.

Graicunas, V.A. (1933), 'The Manager's Span of Control', in *The Bulletin of the International Management Institute*, March.

Harrison, F. and Lock, D. (2004), *Advanced Project Management: A Structured Approach*, 4th edn, Aldershot: Gower.

Hartman, F.T. (2000), *Don't Park Your Brain Outside*, Newtown Square, PA.: Project Management Institute.

Huczyinski, A. and Buchanan, D.A., (2001), *Organizational Behaviour: An Introductory Text*, 4th edn, Hemel Hempstead: Prentice-Hall.

Kerzner, H. (2003), *Project Management: A Systems Approach to Planning, Scheduling and Controlling*, 8th edn, New York: Wiley.

Meredith, J.R. and Mantel, S.J. Jr (2003), *Project Management: A Managerial Approach*, 5th edn, New York: Wiley.

8 Accelerating the Project: Controlling Progress and Costs

This chapter deals with the principal activities of the project manager in controlling the project. It is extremely unlikely that a project will go entirely as planned. What should the project manager do if tasks take longer than expected? What if additional essential work is discovered? Suppose the organization assigns expert resources to another project, increases the scope, raises the expectation of quality yet even at the same time wants the project delivered sooner than planned? And – something that most project managers are entirely unprepared for – what if the project progresses more rapidly or more cheaply than expected? Will Parkinson's Law (Parkinson, 1958) then be allowed to operate, so that the 'work expands to fill the time available'?

Much is written and spoken about project control, yet the subject is not universally well understood. There are many misconceptions about what the project manager can, cannot, should or should not do to control costs and progress. Accordingly this chapter explores the nature of project control and, in the process, dispels some of the prevalent myths.

COST CONTROL: A MYTH EXPLODED

Consider a typical project. The project manager is expected to make regular reports of costs and progress to senior management and others. Cost reporting is frequently mistaken for cost control in this context. The main reason why cost *reporting* is not cost *control* is that it takes place after the event, when the money has already been spent or, worse, wasted.

Every project has an intrinsic cost. If the estimators have done their job properly, that intrinsic cost should lie close to the cost budget. It is the cost for which the project should be completed provided that all the work goes well and no unauthorized changes are allowed. However, our project manager is expected to make regular reports of project costs and progress, which often means that a 'project accountant' is engaged to monitor and report the costs, all broken down and set out according to their relevant tasks. But the project cannot be completed at less than its intrinsic cost. All that the project accountant can do is report, historically, what has been spent. And the project accountant him- or herself has to be employed and paid a not inconsiderable salary to do that. So, in this project, cost collection and reporting has made a *certain* addition to project costs without making any cost saving. The function has added cost with no corresponding value.

Of course, costs must be collected and analysed for accounting purposes. Historical cost records of recent past projects are valuable as comparisons when the time comes to estimate the costs of similar projects in the future. But an accounts department already exists to perform all these cost collection duties, and the code of accounts should enable the computer to filter, sort and report. When a project manager seeks to control costs by engaging one or more project accountants, all he or she is doing is attempting in vain to manage the project *costs* whilst losing sight of the need to manage the project *benefits*.

'But', we can hear our readers cry, 'surely the sponsor will expect to get cost and progress reports?' Of course, that is quite true. But those reports can be clearly and quickly produced, without the need to employ special cost and progress engineers or project accountants, because we have planned our project around obvious recognition events and value flashpoints. So we need base our reports only on the achievement (or non-achievement) of those.

'But', we can hear our more persistent and vociferous readers cry, 'surely earned value analysis is a potent cost control weapon?' Well, actually, no, it is not. The advantage of earned value analysis over plain historic costing is that it seeks to provide answers to the following two questions:

1. For what we have actually achieved, how much have we spent compared with our original cost estimate?
2. For what we have actually spent, how much have we achieved compared with what we said we would achieve for that amount of money?

If 'achievement' is seen merely as the accomplishment of planned tasks – as it so often is – earned value analysis is simply tracking expenditure of money against expenditure of effort against plan. It enhances the focus on cost measurement, and whatsoever we measure we get. Worse still, earned value analysis is labour-intensive and adds considerably to the costs of project administration. It can highlight poor cost and progress performance and, if that triggers corrective action, it has some purpose and merit. Earned value analysis cannot, however, be regarded as a principal means of cost control.

To make earned value really mean earned *value*, achievements must be directly translatable to savings, revenue or increased asset value. Without the Isochron concepts of recognition events and value flashpoints, it is rare indeed to see such a specific relationship. In the Isochron methods of benefit tracking we measure just such a relationship, recording and controlling true value.

So, is project cost control a myth – something with which we need not concern ourselves? Of course not. It is the process, not the intent that needs questioning. So what practical and effective measures can the project manager take to keep costs within budget without making the mistake of hiring costly additional staff? The answer to this question requires, first, that we can identify the cost constituents of a typical IT or business change project. In summary, these are as follows:

1. *Use of internal resources*. These costs include, for example, the notional cost (lost opportunity cost or indirect cost) of using the organization's staff, working accommodation, meeting rooms, training accommodation and so on.
2. *Purchases of third-party services*. These might include, for example contractors, trainers, advisors and consultants.
3. *Purchases of tangible goods and supplies*. These might include servers, communications equipment, desktop computers, furniture, buildings and accommodation (including external meeting and training accommodation).

The greatest project costs will typically fall into the first of the above categories. In industrial projects, timesheet procedures collect and allow measurement of internal direct labour costs. However, in the kinds of business change and IT projects with which we are concerned, the internal costs are usually notional, because the staff and resources are part of the organization's existing fixed costs. Timesheet and other cost collection methods do not apply, and the costs are not counted or analysed. Yet, when the project is under way, the business will frequently be aware of the impact caused by recruiting and retaining the many expert staff needed to run a project, and the time lost by some of its best business experts when they are temporarily assigned to advise the project team.

The next largest cost is the purchase of third-party resources. Of course, this and the purchase of tangible goods can, at the expense of adding time to the project, be *minimized* (but not *controlled*) by making all high-value purchases against competitive tenders. For certain high-value contracts in the public sector this is unavoidable owing to the EU Public Procurement Directives (for further information visit http://www.ogc.govuk/index.asp?id=1000084). Providing suppliers with well-considered and unambiguous purchase specifications will minimize the need for subsequent purchase order amendments (which always threaten to increase costs). Bid summary and analysis procedures should ensure that the chosen suppliers are competent and financially sound. Cost control of these purchases takes place before or just as the costs are committed – not afterwards when it would be too late. It requires no additional staff. Although the project manager must be acquainted with these methods, the existing procurement management would normally be primarily responsible for seeing them carried out.

Attempting to limit purchase costs by contractual methods is a very worthy thing to do. Fixed price contracts can remove some risk of overspending but when, as in many IT and business change projects, the work content cannot be specified with complete accuracy, the buyer is forced to enter into a schedule of rates or cost-plus kind of contract. In any rate-based agreement, there is always a temptation to accept the bid that offers the lowest rates. However, outlined below are three case histories that illustrate why the lowest rates quoted may not offer the best value. The first case was real and the other two are based on real-life experience.

Case 1

One of us (DL) was once responsible for engaging hundreds of engineers and designers from time to time to augment the permanent staff of a British Midlands engineering company. All contracts were let on the basis of hourly rates, because it was generally not possible to define tasks in sufficient detail to ask for fixed price quotations. Rates varied widely from one agency to another, so that the highest rate was double the rate quoted by the 'cheapest' agency. A shortage of available skilled people in the area meant that four or five agencies had to be used, regardless of their quoted rates. It was found that the 'cheaper' agencies always charged more time than the higher-rate agencies for equivalent tasks, so that the prices actually paid per task varied little from one agency to another. However, the higher-charging agencies tended to give a better level of service: there were fewer invoice quibbles, and they supplied more highly skilled people who needed less supervision and produced a faster delivery.

Case 2

A project manager wished to hire the services of a company which was expert in the Answer-to-All database. He was unable to enter into a fixed price arrangement, but knew that this particular phase of his project would last for nine months. Calculated on the basis of a normal five-day week, and allowing for various holidays, this represented 180 working days. He estimated that two agency people would be needed full-time, so that the total estimated workload was 360 man-days. Competitive tenders were sought for the provision of these two people. Three quotations were received, in the following sums:

1. £900 per man-day (an expected project cost of £324 000)
2. £600 per man-day (an expected project cost of £216 000)
3. £550 per man-day (an expected project cost of £198 000).

Horrified by these predicted total costs, the project manager and his sponsor chose the lowest of the three tenders. However, when the work started, the two contracted individuals proved to be mere journeymen of the required skills. Progress slipped so badly that double the expected time was needed, so that the eventual cost rose to double the original estimate. In fact, the costs reached £396 000, considerably more than the cost estimated for the highest bidder, yet the database design was poor. Worse still, this work delayed completion of the whole project and led to an increase of £1.5 million in all the other third-party costs.

Case 3

In a case similar in all other respects to Case 2, the project manager and sponsor bravely chose the highest bidder. The contractor chosen was an acknowledged master of Answer-to-All database design. In fact, such confidence existed in this contractor that it is questionable whether a competitive tendering process was necessary. When the work started, the contractor's staff were able to identify smarter ways to design the database than was originally envisaged, and they were able to keep on schedule throughout their task. The job was done comfortably within the 360 man-days estimate and the costs were kept within the estimated £324 000. The result was a robustly designed database, of high quality, delivered within the time and cost estimates. As in all project work, timely completion of this task ensured that no delay was caused to any other project task.

Moral

It is evident from the three cases cited above that progress and expenditure are not controlled by managing costs directly or by monitoring them closely. They are driven directly by the interplay between the skill level of the resource deployed, the approach used by the resource and the focus on completing what is expected within the required deadline. Intuitively, we know this. Yet very often we fail to act on it. The golden rule of cost and time control is:

> When a project is slipping, cut out the novices, apprentices and journeymen from the teams (that is, the training and management overhead). Let the masters and craftsmen go faster and deliver higher quality. In so doing, cut the costs (fewer people for fewer days), raise the quality and deliver earlier.

A project manager has many brakes on a project. This device is one of his or her best accelerators.

THE PROJECT MANAGER'S ROLE IN CONTROLLING THE PROJECT

A glance at Figure 8.1 will show that the project manager operates in an environment where the parameters of budgeted cost, available time, quality and project scope are determined by the business. The project manager can have no authority to change any of those parameters or travel any of the east, west or southerly routes shown in Figure 8.1. The project manager's role, therefore, is threefold:

1. to choose and use only people who have the necessary skills;
2. to ensure that the approach to technical solutions is pragmatic and flexible;
3. to focus the activities of the project team on getting the job done or, rather, on the expected project benefits.

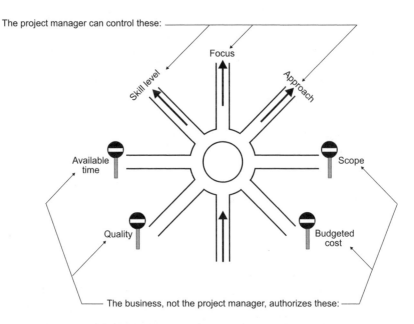

Figure 8.1   Navigating to achieve the expected outcomes

SKILLS MANAGEMENT

Many hands make light work. There's another myth waiting to be detonated. On a farm, in a rice paddy field or on a construction site the proverb might hold good. In business change projects and in the kitchen the more appropriate proverb is that too many cooks will spoil the broth. There are at least two good reasons for this:

1. The more people who work on a project, the greater will be the difficulty and complexity of communication. This was discussed in Chapter 7. The easiest team to manage, and the one that produces the project outcomes fastest, is the lean, all-skilled task force.
2. Too often, increasing the size of a team by bringing in more people will dilute the collective skill bank because the newcomers will not have the skills needed to start, continue and conclude their tasks unaided or without error.

Choosing people with the appropriate skills

The arguments in this section apply particularly to business change and IT projects where the sponsor expects successful outcomes in the shortest possible time. Here we have to assume that the project manager has the authority to choose the people who will work on the team. Of course, there might be limitations caused by a scarcity of people with the relevant skills who are actually employed in the company. However, senior management should not impose additional limitations on the project manager by preventing him or her from choosing the best possible people to join the project team. In this, as in so many other matters, the project manager should be able to rely on the full support of senior company management. The cooperation of departmental managers might also be needed if they are asked to release valuable, skilled people to work temporarily on the project.

In the ideal project team every person will have the skill and experience needed to work unaided, without supervision, and to use their imagination, drive and intelligence to overcome problems by making personal assumptions or choices of action without having to seek assistance from the project manager or others.

For those who remain unconvinced, consider the following true story. A project manager was concerned that her small team would not be able to finish the project on time. Her team comprised four skilled people and two junior trainees. She was asked what would happen if she released the two trainees from the team. 'Oh well,' came the immediate response, 'that would save us time, we could get on without interruptions from the trainees, and I'm sure we could get this project done on time.' So, what happened in practice? Senior management, in their profound wisdom, refused to release more skilled people to work on the project or to remove the two trainees from the project team. Instead, they did what they thought was giving the project manager support by drafting in two more trainees. That decision actually delayed the project further, and it ran even more over time and budget.

The project team on a critical business change project is no place for novices, trainees, apprentices, journeymen or anyone else who will need constant supervision and direction. Of course, such people must gain experience and training, and it is well recognized (by Celinsky, 1998, for example) that training on-the-job is far more effective than sending people on external seminars and courses. As we suggested earlier in this chapter, however, this strategy causes a severe drain on time and cost.

Novices, apprentices and journeymen take up valuable time of the masters in the project in supervision and instruction. They produce 'wrong first time' results and generate rework. The structural weaknesses in quality that they induce make this a *very* expensive way to train people. Perhaps it is these pressures to reduce costs and increase productivity that have caused apprenticeship schemes to die out in the manufacturing and construction.

If growing and developing skills in the context of projects is more critical and valuable to the organization than achieving the project's objectives, then the cost and time of the project should be generously increased and the expectations of quality reduced. Training and experience on-the-job can be given on projects where the cost and time targets are liberal. Otherwise people identified for development in the skills needed for projects should be kept aside from project work until they reach craftsman skill level through full and proper training with practical exercises.

APPROACH TO SOLUTIONS

In our private lives we tend not to allow things to get in the way of achieving our personal objectives. We do not readily allow ourselves to starve or fail to get some pleasure out of life! We do this by being determined and committed to achieving our ends and being very flexible about the solutions we use to get them. We would not, for example, miss a meal just because our preferred shop is closed. We would not think twice about going to a different one, and would even use one we really didn't like or eat food we would normally avoid if it meant not going hungry. The greatest obstacle to getting what we want is to become fixated on a single way of achieving it. Just occasionally we see children experimenting with this, going hungry or without because the food is not a preferred or familiar solution to satiating their hunger. But, as they become adults, they learn differently.

It should be just the same with projects in business. A project team needs to be clear and resolute about achieving what is expected of it. Isochron maintains that the outcomes should be non-negotiable. In order to meet such unforgiving demands, agility needs not only to be allowed but also to be encouraged in the solutions used to attain the outcomes.

An IT example

Flexibility, agility and lateral thinking are especially important where IT is concerned. It is too easy to be so attracted to the utility of a piece of technology that we let it define the outcome for us, so that the solution and the outcome become bound together.

A business might see a particularly attractive eProcurement system that draws its attention to expensive inefficiencies in its current procurement function. The supplier's sales team may be eager to suggest that their system's particular characteristics are indispensable if big savings are to be gained in procurement.

As a result, the business is persuaded to start a project to acquire and implement the eProcurement system. Getting the system installed has now become the intended outcome – the purpose of the project.

Various things can go wrong with the project. These might, perhaps, include the following:

- Data are unexpectedly difficult to migrate.
- The business is too busy to explain its rules and requirements, so that these are not tailored into the system.
- The eProcurement system itself has faults or deficiencies.

To overcome these difficulties, people start to work harder and longer and more expensively at getting the system installed and handed over. Pressure starts to grow to meet the delivery time on which the business and its procurement department have made plans. But wait! Suppose we ask the business some key questions:

1. Before you were told about the eProcurement system did you have any plans to improve procurement efficiency?
2. What deadlines does the business really have? What would actually happen if the new system were taken off the critical path?
3. What improvements to procurement efficiency could you make in advance of getting the new system, and what savings could be made without it?
4. Are there any other eProcurement systems that, even at this late stage, would give a simpler, cheaper and more practical solution to the perceived need?

In other words, the *true* goal is to buy more efficiently. It's true that the IT solution drew the business's attention to the issue. It's also true that when the IT is delivered and successfully implemented it will underpin and sustain improvements in procurement efficiency. But, right now, the project doesn't have to be hung up on the IT. There are many other possible solutions, any of which might meet what is really our critical goal. The eProcurement 'shop' may be temporarily closed, but that doesn't mean that the business must go hungry. The project can still bring food to the business, perhaps sooner and more cheaply, in the meantime.

In project terms this means that a project manager, aided and supported by the steering committee and sponsor, should not only constantly ask 'What could I be doing concurrently?' but also 'Time out – is there a better and smarter way of delivering the project outcomes (the recognition events)? Is there a better approach?' Such 'time-outs' should be regular and quite frequent, and openly lead to change management incidents and replanning.

Most importantly it should be recognised that IT is unforgiving. It requires every *t* to be crossed and every *i* to be dotted, or it will spread mayhem at megabits per second, possibly bringing sections of the business to a grinding halt. We don't say that IT in projects should be avoided – absolutely the reverse – but, wherever possible, IT should be taken off the critical path and attained in good time and quality.

PROJECT FOCUS

Most project managers are appointed to a project organization that either exists or has been mapped out for them. The most fortunate project manager in this respect will be provided with a team or task force organization in which all the members work only on the project and report directly (or through their functional managers) to the project manager. Project organization structures were discussed at greater length in Chapter 7, but it is relevant to note here that the collective minds in a dedicated project team or task force can more easily be focused on the project and its benefits than is possible in any other kind of organization.

Whatever the organization, however, the project manager has to generate enthusiasm, display confidence and competence, and generally earn the respect and willing cooperation of all the people involved. The personality of the project manager is a crucial factor in the focus and control of a project. Leadership – knowing where to go next, conviction, an infectious certainty of success – hugely improves the probability of meeting expectations.

Some of the best project managers also communicate simple principles on which complexity can structure itself. They manage forcefully and decisively based on the principles they have established and seldom hesitate in direction. Team members can find space within this structure to do things in the way in which they work best, secure in the knowledge that they are conforming with the overall essentials of the project.

The project manager can and should 'walk the floor' to see that the principles are being adhered to, to listen and note what is actually happening, and to communicate his or her confidence in the project's success. This process should save the need for a significant number of the meetings that can otherwise absorb the time of the project manager and other project staff.

The establishment of such simple principles is helped if the end goals of the project are constantly kept in the view of everyone involved. We tend to think of projects moving forwards from a start point around preparation and planning through design, build and test towards handover and finishing. This 'forecasting' approach has a very significant flaw. We inevitably encounter more detail as we work forwards, and complexity will grow. Unless all the parties to the project share a clear definition of what is relevant and what is irrelevant the detail and complexity can, and usually does, grow endlessly, leading to slippage and inflation of costs.

It is vital to be able to distinguish between essential and non-essential work as the project progresses and to be immediately able to halt digression and irrelevant work in its tracks. A technique that works well in this respect is backcasting (described in Chapter 4). The first step is to construct a clear view of how achievement of the project's expectations will be judged. A clear and precise way of doing this is to use recognition events (defined and described in Chapter 1). The project plan is then built around the turning points essential to delivering these recognition events.

The project team (and the business users and everyone else involved) is made familiar with the recognition events and constantly reminded that their task is to make them happen. As fast as detail is discovered and events distract from the plan the project manager can intervene to stop and direct effort and cost towards enabling the recognition events to be achieved.

TIME IS DEEP – NOT LONG: OPTIMIZING CONCURRENCY

What do we mean by deep time? In this context 'deep' refers to the front-to-back dimensions of an object, not to mineshafts or ocean fathoms. Isochron uses the expression 'Time is deep – not long' to emphasize the need for the project manager to progress the project by viewing tasks across the depth of the plan, rather than looking only along its sequential paths. The benefits of this approach become apparent when a team member becomes free to work on a new task but the constraints in the critical path network indicate that no new task can be started.

Every experienced project manager knows that the logic of critical path networks is never entirely accurate. One can usually find some tasks, or at least substantial parts of them, that can be started even when the network diagram clearly indicates that they cannot begin until all their predecessor tasks have been completely finished. To some extent, precedence diagramming (described in Chapter 4) can overcome this problem and indicate tasks that can be planned to overlap or run concurrently. However, even if the planner's intentions were entirely accurate and well considered before the project began, all planning notation, without exception, is limited in what it can communicate. The manager of any project where time is important (and that really means *all* projects) must always be on the lookout for work that can be brought forward, examining the complete list of remaining tasks and asking about each task 'Why can't this task be started today?'. In most cases the network logic will prove true but there will usually be a small, but valuable, number of tasks on which at least some work can be done.

The concurrency of fast-tracking does introduce a risk that some work will have to be done again, when work on other project tasks releases new or changed information. But provided that the project manager exercises skill and judgement in choosing which tasks to bring forward, the risk of rework will be more than balanced by the time saved, and in bringing the project's value flashpoints closer.

CONCLUSION

This chapter should be of great cheer to project managers. It suggests that to countermand the brake pedal that an organization and chance can put upon a project, there is an accelerator pedal, using reskilling, agility in solutions, refocusing and optimizing concurrency. We affirm that strong and positive leadership by managers with clear and simple principles greatly improve a project's chances of success. Important strong measures can be taken, such as challenging apparent essentials and taking some of them off the critical path, that can abruptly lift the burden from everyone involved and make the intractable become tractable once more.

The practical approaches set out in this chapter are used unconsciously in our everyday lives for survival. But they are not obvious to us in the organizational environment, possibly because projects at work are not so much about our own survival as someone else's (that remote legal entity called the company or the department). If we are not as agile or responsible as perhaps we could be, then we allow ourselves to feel that responsibility is shared, and not ours alone. Failure will not hurt us personally. This chapter suggests that if we are to get more pleasure from our project achievements at work, we would do well to treat projects at work in the same way that we approach projects at home, with a personal commitment to the outcome that transcends the means.

REFERENCES AND FURTHER READING

Celinski, D. (1998) 'Training', Chapter 63 in *The Gower Handbook of Management*, 4th edn, Aldershot: Gower.

Lock, D. (2003), *Project Management*, 8th edn, Aldershot: Gower.

Parkinson, C. Northcote (1958), *Parkinson's Law or the Pursuit of Progress*, London: John Murray.

9 Managing Changes to the Project

Whilst the whole purpose of the project is to change the organization in some way, projects themselves are vulnerable to change. There are many kinds of changes and many reasons why they cannot always be avoided. Changes are usually thought of as unwelcome and disruptive, but change is not necessarily bad. The essence of managing project change is to treat the *ends* as non-negotiable and to be agile and flexible in changing the *means*. Unforeseeable events in the future of the project can be accommodated by changing the solution, the approach or the capability of the resources.

WHEN IS A CHANGE NOT A CHANGE?

Some changes need neither managing nor any of the procedures outlined in this chapter. That statement could have some project management purists throwing up their hands in horror, or rushing for their tranquillizer pills. But a moment's thought and a simple example should restore calm in the camp.

Jim has been working for several weeks on the design of a customer invoicing procedure that is to be introduced as part of a project. Everyone makes mistakes: Jim is no exception and he makes his full share. However, he has a fertile and innovative brain, so that he can be forgiven a few false starts. He is halfway through this particular task when he realizes, with some dismay, that he has forgotten to allow for some invoices for overseas customers that will have to show currency exchange rates and conversions. There is no question that, to rectify this mistake, part of Jim's work will have to be done again and that this might delay completion of this task by two weeks. In order to avoid delay to the project, Jim must change some of his plans to find a faster way to do some of the work and still meet the deadline.

But is this a change to the project objectives? No, it is not, because the original scope and intention of the project as outlined in the business case and the PID have not been affected. All that has happened is that Jim has veered off-course, realized the error of his ways and changed his plan – *how* he is going to do the work – so that he gets back on the right track before it is too late and before he has issued any specification or other document to another person, group, department or organization.

The converse of this argument suggests a definition of changes that do demand a special management procedure. These are changes to any specification or other document *already approved and issued to authorize work*. Documents, in this context, mean any document from the PID downwards. A change to the PID is likely to imply a change to the basic scope and intended purpose of the project. Changes to lower-level work instructions can disrupt work in progress, add costs or result in the scrapping of work already done (along with the associated sunk costs).

Changes in relation to the project life cycle

A change made during the conceptual stage of a project might affect a few documents and calculations but little else. A statement, such as 'our new building needs to be ten per cent bigger than we first thought', has far less impact during the conceptual phase of a project than much later, when the walls are up and the roof is on. A change made when the project is nearing completion could mean, in the worst possible case, scrapping a large part of the work already done and starting again. Changes made later in the life cycle of a project invariably cost more than early changes because of the amount of completed work and sunk costs put at risk. This is illustrated in Figure 9.1. As far as the inconvenience, disruption and additional cost caused by a given change is concerned, later is always greater.

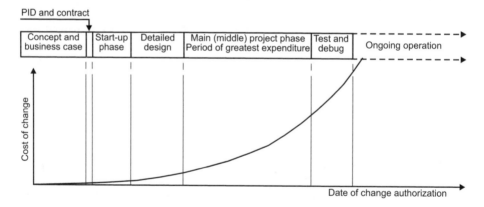

Figure 9.1   The cost of a given change in relation to a typical project life cycle

Design freeze

Many companies, recognizing that late changes can have far greater impact on project costs and progress than very early changes, identify a point in the project life cycle at which all but essential changes should be rejected and declare a 'design freeze' or condition of 'stable design'. There is an important distinction to be made between a design freeze of the required project outcomes and a design freeze of the means or solutions by which those outcomes are to be achieved. If the solution is frozen and unforeseen events subsequently occur, the sponsors must accept that the outcome will be different from their expectations. If, on the other hand, the project outcomes are frozen, then a change of solution may yet deliver expected outcomes. Because it is the outcomes that provide the returns that justify the investment in the project, the outcomes will almost always take precedence over the choice of solution.

A design freeze should not be declared so early as to stifle innovation in design solutions, but it should not be delayed beyond the point where a design change would have significant negative impact on the project by causing work done outside the design group to be scrapped and restarted.

There is always a tendency among some keen technologists to strive for perfection at the expense of a more practicable solution – a situation sometimes described as 'allowing the best to become the enemy of the good'. It is occasionally necessary to call 'Time!' in the design process, announce a design freeze and allow the main thrust of the project to proceed.

CHANGE PROCEDURES

The project as a contract

Isochron points out that treating a project as a contract between the project team and the organization opens up a vast area of expertise for managing change – that of contract management and law. Social and economic activity is dominated by countless contracts, ranging from the large to the trivial. We are all extremely familiar with managing contracts and are unconsciously competent in all the skills required. A whole branch of the law is devoted to contracts, and the principles are very well established.

In law, a contract exists between two parties where a number of factors are present. The most basic of these is that 'consideration' should be exchanged. Consideration is usually money exchanged for service. For example, in employment the employee receives a salary and other benefits in return for his or her service. A purchase is another form of contract. A retail shop gives goods to the customer in return for which the customer gives money to the shop. Construction work is governed by a contract: a builder constructs a building in return for which a customer pays money for the work.

Whilst engineering and manufacturing projects are normally treated as contracts, it is very rare indeed for businesses to perceive their internal change and IT projects to be contracts, because both parties – the sponsoring business and the change and IT team – appear to be in the same organization and on the same side. However, such projects are contracts because the buyer (the organization) is spending or investing money in the project (consideration), in return for which the project team delivers the required outcomes (return consideration). The project team plans, designs, builds and delivers a result, in return for which the organization or buyer provides budget and resources. If you bring out the contract nature of such internal projects you will immediately be able to tap into a great deal of experience and established procedure to control any changes in the terms and conditions.

It is a fortunate coincidence that the terms and conditions of a project are well covered in the contents of a PID (project initiation document or project charter). Consider the following properties of a PID:

- It sets out the objectives and outcomes required by the organization (the buyer or investor).
- It sets out the costs and resources – how much they expect to pay for the project.
- It describes in some detail what the project team is going to deliver for this investment – the 'deliverables' – and what is expected of the deliverables (the quality tests).
- It describes the intentions of the parties in terms of:
    - who is going to perform what roles
    - what procedures are going to be used to control the project
    - how progress is to be reported and managed
    - what is expected to happen at what time (the plan)
    - what risks the parties foresee from the outset.
- It explains what will happen if things change from what is anticipated and how the changes will be managed.

Although it may not be a formal legal document, the PID does conform in almost every way to a legal contract.

Once we become familiar with the idea that a project is a contract and that the PID is the contract document, a great deal of the management of change in a project becomes much clearer. Suddenly the role of the steering committee is not to focus on progress and risks alone. It does not need to tediously study and wring its collective hands over slippage and complex technical reports. It is there to manage the project contract. Thus the steering committee's agenda is continuously dictated by the PID. The questions it should ask are:

- Have the objectives and outcomes required by the organization changed?
- Has there been an alteration in the costs and resources made available?
- Is there any change in what the project team is going to deliver for this investment?
- What do the 'quantity surveyor' and the 'civil engineer' (the quality assurer of the project) report about the quality of the work?
- Are there any changes in the intentions of the parties in terms of who is going to perform what roles, what procedures are going to be used to control the

project, how progress is to be reported and managed, what is expected to happen when (the plan), and what risks the parties foresee?

With this all information the steering committee has to do what any one of us would do with the many countless formal and informal contracts we manage. It must reach agreement on any changes and modify the contract – the PID – accordingly.

Change requests

Accepting that a project is a contract, it follows that a process is needed to capture and track changes. Any person, regardless of seniority, should be allowed to request a change. Some change requests, at least in their early stages, can be regarded in the same light as notes placed in a suggestions box by keen or critical members of staff. There is always a possibility that a proposed change could be beneficial to a project in all respects. Suggestions for improvement should always be encouraged so that opportunities are not lost.

However, most changes cause additional costs and will delay, or at least interrupt, progress. Even changes that at first sight appear to be highly desirable can cause delays, scrapped work and other consequential damage that outweigh their benefits. It would not take very long in the life of a project for a succession of apparently small and harmless changes to result in a significant change in project scope, delayed completion, a badly overspent budget and dissatisfied stakeholders.

So, although suggestions for changes should not be discouraged, there must be a formal, clearly documented and enforced procedure for submitting change requests and for considering whether or not each proposed change should be authorized or disallowed. Further, the originator should at least discuss the outlines of any proposed change with the project manager before completing a change request form, so that time-wasting requests are not issued for changes that would clearly be deleterious and should be ruled out from the start.

The procedure for any change proposal must be initiated by the person (the originator) who thinks that he or she has identified a reason for making a change. The originator should be expected to justify the proposal and put the details in writing, for which a change request form (such as that shown in Figure 9.2) is appropriate. This example is fairly typical of change request forms used in companies from a wide variety of different industries. Most change request forms are relatively straightforward to initiate, and this example is no exception. The originator is asked to describe and justify the request, and space is allowed later on the form to record the management decision.

In our example, the originator or, if necessary, another person assigned to assess the change request, is expected to allocate a change priority level, and to estimate the severity of the impact that the change would have on the project. Figure 9.3 illustrates factors that can influence these priority and impact classifications. Changes that have high priority or urgency or very high desirability are strong contenders for acceptance. Changes that are simply desirable, but which would cause a negative impact would generally have to be rejected.

Request for change		Serial number:		
Change name:		Priority (circle whichever applies)		
		High	Medium	Low
Requested by:	Assigned to::	Date Submitted:		

Description of proposed change:

Reason for the change (benefits):

Implications of not making the change (safety, reliability, costs etc.)

Who needs to be consulted and what are the contractual implications?

Estimated impact of this change (tick one box) ⟶ Low ☐   Medium ☐   High ☐

DECISION

If authorized, specify action here:

If rejected, give reasons here:

Authorized/rejected by:	Date:

Figure 9.2   A change request and control form

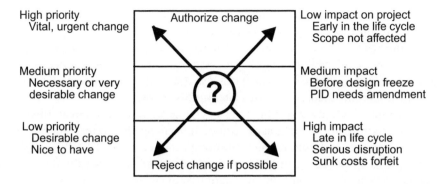

High priority
  Vital, urgent change

Medium priority
  Necessary or very
  desirable change

Low priority
  Desirable change
  Nice to have

Authorize change

?

Reject change if possible

Low impact on project
  Early in the life cycle
  Scope not affected

Medium impact
  Before design freeze
  PID needs amendment

High impact
  Late in life cycle
  Serious disruption
  Sunk costs forfeit

Figure 9.3   Project change classification (where no external funding is possible)

Coordination procedure

Changes intended to correct deficiencies in reliability, performance or safety are always high priority and must be dealt with very promptly indeed. However, it is conceivable that even a change designated as desirable and low impact at the time of the request could become high impact if delay in considering the request pushed implementation further along the project life cycle. A request such as 'I would like a thin client architecture rather than desktops' has little impact at the start of a project – it merely involves retyping a couple of words on a specification document. Later, when large quantities of desktops have been purchased, the change might mean paying costs of removal and damages to a supplier and accepting higher prices for the replacement architecture. Later still, however, when the project is finished and everyone has the desktops the request will become high impact, involving expensive withdrawal and write-offs and a delayed project completion and handover. All this serves to demonstrate that even low-priority change requests should at least be considered without delay. The process requires a standardized coordination and progressing procedure to ensure the following:

- Every change request receives prompt and appropriate executive consideration.
- The request is presented for consideration to a competent person or group for approval or rejection.
- If the change is rejected, the originator is informed and given reasons.
- If approved, the change is implemented, both on the project itself and in all affected documents (which might mean amending the PID).
- Every change request is monitored and tracked through all these stages – just as a project task would be.

It is prudent to assign a person or group to monitor every change request and follow it through all stages of approval (or rejection) and implementation. This does not have to be a full-time role and it is usually performed by a junior member of the organization such as a technical clerk, but, ideally, the person should have some procurement contract experience. An organization that has a project support office (PSO) will invariably place responsibility for coordinating its change procedures within that office, which can also deal with any consequential contract administration procedures (outlined later in this chapter).

The usual method for keeping track of change requests through all their stages is for the coordinator to enter each request on a change log (often called a change register) that acts as a kind of diary, allowing each request to be followed day-by-day through all its stages. In addition to assisting with the coordination process, change logs can also become an important part of the project archives, where they provide an audit trail should post-project investigations be needed for any reason. A typical page from a change log is shown in Figure 9.4.

The change board or steering committee

It is not uncommon to find a good deal of confusion about what should and should not be the business of a change board or steering committee. Large volumes of report can be presented, giving the committee members little indication of what is intended for their attention and what action is expected of them. This sometimes leads to meetings with too many attendees, overloaded agendas, evasion of major decisions and interference in minor project issues.

Where the PID is treated as a contract between the organization (the buyer) and the project team (the service deliverer) the position is crystal clear. Any change that would alter the terms of the PID needs to be reported and put on the agenda of the steering committee's next meeting. It is the business of the steering committee to reach agreement on any changes and modify the contract, and then communicate the changes. Any other changes should be managed within the project, bearing in mind that the project should include both IT and the business.

Given a contract management role, the board or committee needs members that will give it the following capabilities:

1. authority to change the project contract, including the investment (budget and resources), required outcome and any contracts with external suppliers;
2. ability to evaluate the quality of the work independently of those delivering the project;
3. understanding of the implications of progress or the lack of it, and of risks;
4. expertise to understand and evaluate optional solutions put to it.

The level of authority needed means that the committee *has* to have the sponsor present at every meeting. Where – as is not uncommon – the sponsor does not have the authority to make major spending decisions on the spot, a main board director needs to be a member of the committee. In projects where the commitment of the sponsor and director wanes during the project and they cease to attend, or under-powered deputies are sent, the contract drifts, progress slows dramatically

Project:

Notes:

(1) H = High
    M = Medium
    L = Low

(2) R = Request rejected
    A = Requested action approved
    I = Impact analysis requested

(3) Brief description of the action undertaken or the outcome of impact analysis.

Serial number	Date of change request	Change requested by:	Priority (Note 1)	Date assessed	Result (Note 2)	Approved by:	Actions assigned to:	Estimated start date	Action result (Note 3)	Date change completed

Figure 9.4   A change log (or change register) page

and costs start to rise out of control. Sponsors and directors should understand that their non-attendance at a steering committee meeting has a direct impact on costs. Those costs can be so great that they are out of all proportion to the time taken by the meeting and the other work of committee members that may be displaced.

Where the project managers or team members are allowed to report to the committee they will inevitably be biased in favour of continuing progress. Yet it is common for the project manager to be the main source and presenter of progress information to a steering committee, much like allowing a building contractor to report the quality and progress of its own work without comment from any independent engineer and quantity surveyor. Construction projects have civil engineers and quantity surveyors who have the skill and understanding to check that the work is being done correctly and to the right specifications. Without their independent supervision, and nagging, snagging powers to force rework and report non-conformance, such projects cannot succeed. IT and business change projects need the same function to be performed, and it is usually labelled QA (quality assurance). It is essential that the QA is independent of the project team.

The need to understand the implications of financial decisions means that a senior representative of the organization's finance function should also sit on the committee. The committee may have to consider the impact and approve a change to the required outcome, so it is essential that the head or heads of the business areas impacted by the project should be present. Where the project involves significant contracts with external suppliers, a representative of the organization's purchasing or procurement function must be present to advise on impacts of project change on the contracts.

Lastly, but by no means least, the committee needs to have direct input from the primary representative of the delivery side of the project – the project manager (or managers, if it is a programme board). It is common practice for the project manager to be asked to make the main report on progress, but a better and more objective report will flow from an independent process set up to provide frequent dashboard-style updates. This ensures a lack of bias and also prevents the project manager being diverted from the essential task of managing the project into unproductive report writing.

For a very large project in which PID (contract) change requests are frequent, the board or steering committee must meet on a regular and equally frequent basis. It is often difficult to persuade the senior members of the committee to give up time for such meetings. This is particularly true where poor definition of the committee's role, too many attendees and the wrong sort of reports cause meetings to take up a quarter or even half a day. Well-organized and well-chaired project steering meetings, where the agenda is properly focused, can be held within time-slots as short as one hour. The scale of expenditure, the value of the benefits and the cost of failure for very large IT and business change projects is usually so great that the priority for time is justified.

In very small projects, where changes are infrequent, the change coordinator might simply be expected to consult the project manager or a member of the steering committee for a decision. What is important is that the route to authorization or rejection is written into project procedures and made known to everyone working on the project. Once established, the change procedure must be operated without fear, favour or exception.

Every project will have moments when a decision affects a number of current urgent actions. Requests for very high-priority or emergency changes must be dealt with as soon as possible, which means that the change coordinator will not have time to wait for a scheduled steering committee meeting. A fast track must be preplanned, which is able to escalate a request for authority up to the highest level that might be required. This arrangement should anticipate the need to speak directly with the project sponsor or a main board director (or to a deputy with their full delegated authority) even when they are out of the country. The absence of anyone with the necessary authority at a key moment is one of the principal causes of project slippage and overspending.

Change decisions

The organization can equally well be the originator of change as the project team. The business objectives may alter as a result of changes in market conditions or regulations. The investment (budget) may be altered as a result of priority changes and financial tactics. Key delivery personnel might be withdrawn from the project. Change should not be seen as confined to delivery-side problems and slippage.

Project responsibility is commonly passed off to a delivery team (often IT) who are subsequently held responsible for all needs. This is ineffectual and irresponsible management, often symptomatic of a blame culture. For management to justify the investment that an organization is making in them, a mature contract management approach must be established between the equal parties of investor and deliverer. Change decisions should be made, therefore, by the steering committee. However, to enable the committee to operate efficiently, recommended courses of action should be prepared before the committee meets and then put to the committee with compelling, or at least persuasive, substantiation. The change, its impact and estimated cost should be recorded on a change request form that accompanies the change log. The change request form will become part of the audit trail of changes to the PID.

Follow-up

If a change has been rejected, the originator must be informed. This is an act of courtesy which, if ignored, can cause dissatisfaction and greater resentment than having the change rejected. The usual and most convenient method for providing feedback to the originator is to send her or him a copy of the change request form, bearing the decision and the reasons for it. The change coordinator will record the fate of the rejected change on the change log and close further action on that particular request.

When a change has been approved, with or without restrictions, the original change request form becomes, instead, a change authorization document. When the coordinator distributes copies of the change authorization, the following are typical of the actions that might be initiated:

1. The project sponsor and steering committee are informed.
2. The project team and business managers will try to maintain momentum of work to avoid creating a progress gridlock of the 'I can't until...' variety. They will assume that the common-sense decision will prevail until they get confirmation. They will, however, make a contingency plan for rework in the unlikely event that their assumption should prove to be wrong.
3. The commercial manager or other responsible person will consider the effect on any affected purchase orders or other contractual documents and, where necessary, issue amendments.
4. The project manager will arrange for budgets and work schedules to be amended, as necessary, to incorporate the change.

The change coordinator will ensure that all these steps are followed and, only when they have been all been completed, sign off the change in the change log.

CONTRACT ADMINISTRATION

For most management projects, contract administration actions caused by changes will mean updating or amending the PID. Many small changes will require no such action, since they will not affect the main thrust of the project or significantly affect the budget. They might, however, have more significant effect when considered collectively.

In commercial projects, conducted for an external customer, the question of who shall pay for each change arises. This is usually a fairly cut-and-dried issue, determined as follows:

*   Changes requested by the customer (the organization) should result in formal contract amendments or contract variations, each of which will amend the project budget (usually upwards).
*   Changes generated entirely within the project organization, which might or might not result from design errors, are usually regarded as the sole responsibility of the project organization. The project organization itself must therefore fund these changes and take responsibility for any consequential delays (in the full knowledge that those delays might annoy the customer and attract additional cost penalties).

The situation in internal management change projects is somewhat different from projects carried out by one organization for an external customer, because the question of who should fund each change does not arise (there might be internal disputes concerning the allocation of costs between departments or different companies in a group, but the costs must still come from internal reserves).

As we have already pointed out, in an internal management change and IT project the PID, although it may not have legal force, is nonetheless a contract document. In its business case section it will show the cash flow (which will set out costs and benefit flows month-by-month). This and the associated net present value statements provide a simplified form of ledger for the information of the steering committee. To allow an audit trail of changes the committee must therefore record the original baseline business case and each successive change to the business case when it has been approved.

To prevent 'micro-management' of change, the organization should agree in advance the threshold of change value and impact below which smaller changes will be consolidated into larger changes when they occur. For example, the committee might agree that movements in net present value of less than £1 million, or impacts on the project of less than £10 million, or a delay in breakeven point of less than three months will not be separately recorded but grossed up pending movements above these thresholds.

When Isochron approaches are used, the benefit values will rest on estimates of discrete value flashpoints. Thus the steering committee and finance function will have complete transparency of the impact and history of change on the contract.

If the reserve budget runs out for an internal change management project, the commitment to continue with the project might not be so firm. Indeed, if very serious overspending begins to put the intended project benefits in jeopardy, the business case might have to be re-examined and a brave decision taken to terminate the project, pulling the plug to prevent further good money being sent down the unforgiving drain. The expert project sponsor will recognize a developing catastrophe such as this early enough to cancel or redefine the project before serious damage is done.

However, the principal aim of contract administration is, of course, not to signal project termination but to ensure that the contractual commitments remain valid and up to date, taking into account all changes, and to help the project manager ensure that the project is finished on time and within budget.

CONCLUSION

This chapter has identified the need to treat project changes seriously by establishing a change management procedure and by treating the PID as if it were a legal contract. Any such procedure depends on a formal system for channelling change requests, establishing a person or group to authorize or reject the requests, with the process monitored, logged and followed up by a change coordinator or other suitable person who can ensure that every request proceeds through all stages of the procedure without undue delay. The procedure must ensure that every authorized change does, in fact, get implemented with minimum delay. This means changing not only the actual project work, but also all the associated documentation. The procedure must also provide for the originator to be informed of the reasons for a rejected change.

REFERENCES AND FURTHER READING

Lock, D. (2003), *Project Management*, 8th edn, Aldershot: Gower.

10 *Executing the Business Change*

Construction and other industrial projects change physical things. A very important characteristic of business and IT projects is that their success depends far more on people accepting change. At the very least, that change involves people using new technology and processes if they are to achieve the organization's intended project benefits. Often the change in people's lives is far greater. New and unfamiliar posts may be created and people promoted, moved or demoted to fill them. The posts might be in new locations. New procedures and routines have to be learned and followed. Sometimes the deep structure of the organization has to change and, with it, the culture, so that beliefs, attitudes and behaviours have to alter. Myths and stories may have to be rooted out; the familiar day-to-day language and customs of the organization will alter. Habits and beliefs of a working lifetime that have brought status, security and mental comfort might have to be discarded. This chapter is the first of two about how we make these people-centred changes happen.

No matter how competent we might be at acquiring new buildings, altering accommodation and building complicated new information technology, we must be equally competent in the fields of social and behavioural psychology, both at the individual and organizational level. Time and again we hear of projects (especially government projects) where, even when the technology is delivered, the result goes wrong. In very many projects there is a large, black hole in the management of people change that causes a great deal of distress and non-achievement. This is where IT, facilities management and human resource (HR) management overlap.

ORGANIZATION CHANGES

One of the fastest and easiest ways to start to make changes in the business is to change the organization – that is, change who does what. The result should be evident in the organization chart (or organigram, as it is often called). The functions of each post are implied in the job title and further defined in the job description. A good organigram will show the principal lines of authority and responsibility in its tree structure.

One of the first instincts of senior managers seeking to achieve their objectives is to alter posts and responsibilities. Consider the impact of creating a new post and appointing or recruiting a person to fill it. It's a bit like installing a new machine tool in a production line. All of a sudden, new procedures are being carried out that were not done before. The whole sequence of production will change and the results will alter accordingly.

Staying with the production analogy, removing one machine tool from a plant will throw load on to other parts of the manufacturing facility. Similarly, making a post redundant and sacking a person will not, by itself, make the intended saving in costs. Unless the tasks, authorities and responsibilities that went with that post are also made redundant, the work burden will fall on to others. It might even impair the results that the company wishes to achieve.

A typical senior manager might think, 'All I need to do is to sack some people, create new posts and job definitions and then appoint people into them and I will achieve some of my company's expectations.' That might be true. But what he or she will also do is create a wave of temporary failure in the system and what he or she will *not* do is change the deep structure of the organization.

Frequency of organizational changes

If successive organizational changes are made too frequently the company's functions can sink into chaos. Consider what would happen if we modified the flight control systems of a fighter aircraft while it was in flight. OK, you might say, provided that you give the systems time to bed in before the next change of flight direction is needed the aircraft will remain stable. If you change the systems several times during the performance of a single flight command, however, the behaviour of the aircraft will become unpredictable and chaotic, with a risk that it will 'go in' (as the flight industry euphemistically terms a catastrophic crash).

As a rule of thumb, therefore, Isochron suggests that the cycle time of a change to any organization should be made on a lower frequency than the cycle time of the business function affected. This can be explained, for example, by considering a finance function that runs on an annual cycle. In that case, because the cycle is one year, one should not change the finance organization more than once in any year.

To understand why this is so, imagine a situation where administrators are familiar with the process of producing the annual accounts and budgets. Suppose that a change is made which causes people experienced in this function to be replaced, or authorities are changed, or workloads are increased. There will be a temporary reduction in efficiency of all the many procedures involved as people adjust to their new working patterns. However, the true impact will not be known until the financial year-end has passed and the impact on all the procedures and processes can be assessed.

Now consider what would happen if more than one successive change is made during one financial year. Any flaws in these changes will be compounded before there is a chance to see the impact. As more changes are implemented within the year, the consequences for the year-end become less and less predictable.

The chaos caused by excessively frequent change has become the stuff of legends. Most of us will be familiar with the following passage:

We trained hard, but it seemed that every time we were beginning to form up into teams we would be reorganized. I was to learn later in life that we tend to meet any new situation by reorganizing; and a wonderful method it can be for creating the illusion of progress while producing confusion, inefficiency and demoralization. (Variously attributed to Petronius, 66 AD, or Petronius Arbiter, 210 BC, but probably modern, true author unknown)

CHANGES TO PROCEDURES AND PROCESSES

Frequency of procedural changes

The rule about change frequency in organizations given in the preceding section applies equally to changes in procedures and processes. Procedures and processes are cyclic. Change them more than once during one cycle and the output becomes unpredictable and eventually chaotic. During the early research that underlies many Isochron techniques, one of us (AF) led the construction of a computer application in which the logic could be changed while the application was being run.

Each time the system encountered a permutation of data for which it had no rule, instead of showing an error message and requiring a rerun it paused temporarily and presented the data to the user for a decision about what to do in the new circumstances. When the user had decided which processes to run in this eventuality, the system recompiled itself and carried on running from where it had left off.

Such a system demonstrates second-order dynamics – change to the process of change. Had the application not paused and sought an intelligent redirection and learning, the output would have become random and chaotic. This is obvious when considering a computerized process, but it is equally true of any other process, procedural or organizational change.

Development of design documentation

Procedures and processes have to be designed. Design presupposes a documentation method. Documentation for design has evolved through many phases and fashions. In the 1960s and 1970s discursive text was used with some diagrams to describe the output of systems analysis. A strict form of text called 'pseudo-code' was used to specify the computer programs that had to be written.

Towards the end of the 1970s through into the 1990s, new formal and highly structured methods of analysis and diagramming came into play to describe the decomposition of business functions, the flow of data between functions, the sequence and logic of each iteration of a function and the logical and physical structure of data relations.

By the late 1980s these methods of analysing and diagramming procedures became so exhaustive that, recorded in electronic format by CASE (Computer

Aided Systems Engineering) software tools, they could be automatically translated into computer program code. An advantage was that they also documented very explicitly how the business worked and linked the top-level overview to granular detail with no missing pieces. Unfortunately the work had to be so detailed that many projects died of 'paralysis by analysis', never reaching development let alone implementation.

By the end of the 1990s, perhaps because of the paralysis problem, perhaps because of transfer of attention to Year 2000, or perhaps because of the new fashion for object-oriented programming, these structured methods faded out of use. They were replaced by the still-fashionable RUP (Rational Unified Process), based around an object-oriented view of life.

Object orientation observes that the world is made up of objects, defined relative to one another by the values of their data, each having a behaviour represented by logic. The data and the logic can be represented in computer code. The business view is seen in the form of the objects of which the business consists (workers, workflows, artefacts and activities) and scenarios in the business, analysed into use-cases. This view, though satisfactory for IT people who are building technology, is not how organizations see themselves and shares little language with the business. In most organizations, as a result, there is little documentation of procedures and processes to be changed, other than traditional procedure manuals and increasingly out-of-date structured analysis diagrams.

Large change programmes and projects usually require the creation of schematic pictures that show how the new business will work and how procedures and technology will fit in. These are often akin to pictorial flowcharts and are an effective tool to talk people through the post-change procedures. It can be difficult and time-consuming, however, to relate these pictures to detailed descriptions of how-to-do procedures. What the technology is actually required to do is represented as computer screen designs and dialogues, which are the interface between the people and the applications. RUP can then translate these into scenarios and use-cases. Models which show the logical and physical structures of the data used by the business are still in fashion and used as the basis for designing the computer databases.

FOCUS ON IT

There is an enormous volume of literature on the management of IT projects. However, it cannot be said, that this has led to any radical improvement in the results of the projects as far as business is concerned. There is widespread agreement in the UK that the government's PRINCE 2 (Project In Controlled Environments) methodology represents best practice. However, although PRINCE 2 emphasizes the importance of the business context and the management of business change, it remains fundamentally IT-centric in origin and thinking.

In the late 1960s and 1970s when computers were a relatively new technology, good project practice was to carry out a thorough analysis of the business and business changes up-front and to make sure that both the business and the computing processes were designed as an integrated unit (Lee, 1979). Throughout the 1980s and 1990s projects of any sort seemed to be passed straight over to IT departments, who developed ever more IT-focused project management methodologies. So strong has this move been that it is common to hear people speak nowadays in accusatory terms of 'a lack of business readiness' and the business 'not being ready' to receive the IT. We strongly deplore this trend. As you can see in this book, most of the Isochron methods radically reverse these two decades of misdirection.

For IT to contribute to the efficiency and effectiveness of an organization it is essential to position it as an enabler and not as a self-fulfilling objective. From the perspective of the people in an organization who have to change the performance of their business unit, IT is usually best positioned as a subproject within an overall programme of change.

MANAGING THE MINDSETS

Organizations, like all sorts of communities, grow legends (true, though often caricatured, stories) and myths (untrue stories) about themselves. When people first join an organization they are relatively free of these stories, but as they settle in they learn them and eventually become influenced by them. These legends and myths are particularly important in change management because they tend to be self-fulfilling.

One of us, when teaching project management, often asks groups to say why their projects fail. It is often possible to fill three flipchart sheets with reasons for failure, which the groups proffer readily. The same groups are then asked for reasons why their projects succeed, but in no case has any group ever been able to give any reason for success. Their myth is that their projects always fail, so they have no reason to report for success. These flipchart sheets demonstrate that these people, in typical fashion, know a lot about how failure happens. Thus, in their workplaces, preparations and planning always follow the track that is most familiar to them: the track that leads yet again to failure. So the failure myth is fulfilled and reinforced.

Fortunately it is possible to demonstrate the reverse. Where a myth of *success* is constructed, success starts to be achieved. When, many years ago, one us was working on a statistical analysis of the success of projects in the UK government's Department of Work and Pensions, it became clear that a small number of large projects were widely perceived as being particularly successful. In every successful case the project manager was regarded as maverick – someone who did things radically differently and had the 'brass neck' to override customary procedures. When these people were put in charge of projects, success was expected. So success resulted. Unfortunately, maverick behaviour is not always appreciated.

We may be able to identify things that we do in our private lives where we simply assume that we will succeed, because we always have in the past and expect to continue to do so. However, if we lose that confidence, we start to think that we might fail. When that happens, failure becomes an option and we actually start to fail.

In managing change we have to create a detailed picture of what success would (or rather will) look like. We must then communicate this image widely and thoroughly. This will begin to harness the power of all those people who will be affected in some way by the project (the stakeholders). It is often forgotten that we find it just as hard to forget things as to remember them. A vision of the successful future, represented in this case by the achievement of all the project objectives, can be unforgettable. Once heard, it works away in the unconscious minds of everyone involved, guiding millions of micro-decisions.

The project manager has to nurse this vision of success to make sure that powerfully entrenched failure legends and myths do not rise up and overwhelm it. Apart from being a positive and inspiring leader and radiating certainty in the outcome, the project manager can work out the recognition events and value flashpoints of the vision and then cement them in the project plan. Tasks will then grow on and around the recognition events and so align them with the successful outcome.

The business of 'what if?' scenario planning, which envisages and analyses things that might go wrong, is not redundant, but it should be firmly placed into the risk management function. Possibilities of failure must not be confused with the expected outcome of the project.

EXPERIENCE-RELATED PERFORMANCE

The results that people obtain in their everyday work are directly related to the way they behave in response to events. In turn, the way they behave is directly related to how they feel about events and to what they believe about those events. Two different examples will illustrate this point.

Example 1: Pessimism and a negative outlook

A person might learn that his or her post is to be made redundant at the end of a project in which he or she is taking part. Suppose that, in the past, this person had been through the painful experience of being made redundant. Finding a new job had taken nine anxious months. Self-esteem and confidence had collapsed, and the family had suffered financial hardship and had had to endure a general atmosphere of gloom and despondency.

People who have been through such an experience believe that the same thing will happen again. As a result, they feel both angry and depressed when they learn of a new change. They behave irritably. They even seek a meeting with their manager at which they are very critical of the company and its management. They demand better treatment.

The manager in such a case is upset by the attack and retaliates with annoyance and a strong lecture. As the employee leaves the room, the manager makes a firm mental note not to strive to transfer that awkward individual to another post but instead to arrange dismissal with the minimum deal the company can afford as soon as the opportunity arises. The employee's pessimism, engendered from his painful past experience, has contributed to his own fate in a clear case of a self-fulfilling prophecy.

Example 2: Optimism and a positive outlook

Now imagine that another person, working in similar circumstances to the individual in Example 1, learns that his post will become redundant when the project is finished. This time, however, imagine that this person has been made redundant before but was able to secure another (better) job almost immediately. So with this new job and most of the redundancy benefits still in the bank, this event was one of the best financial things that had ever happened to them. It had even been possible to paint these events to family and friends as a personal success. Consequently when this person hears about the new redundancy there is an expectation that the successful outcome of the previous redundancy will be repeated.

Now let's be a fly on the wall when the manager interviews this person. The employee exudes confidence and is cooperative. The manager is impressed with this positive and constructive attitude, which is displayed both towards the current project and to the future. When the employee has left the room the manager makes a note not to try to keep the employee by transferring him to a stopgap or unsuitable post when the time comes, but instead to arrange for career guidance, assistance in finding another job and the best possible redundancy deal. Thus the same trigger event that happened in Example 1 has produced a completely opposite outcome, based entirely on the person's belief (not fact) about what was likely to happen.

These two examples demonstrate that if, within change management, we can train people to have positive beliefs about the future, a positive outcome is much more likely. It is not certain to happen, of course, and this is where cynics can get in and induce failure. That lack of certainty should be dealt with as a real potential risk, but be attacked positively with contingency plans and opportunity analysis: it should not be allowed to become a self-fulfilling prophecy of failure. The induction of commitment to a successful outcome and positive beliefs about the future will be noticed by observers as a change in attitude. Following from the argument above, changes of attitude are based on communicating new and up-to-date facts, which in turn influence beliefs, and so feelings and thence behaviours and results (see Figure 10.1).

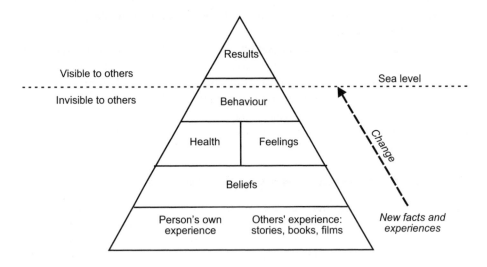

Figure 10.1   Understanding where people are coming from (the iceberg)

PUSH VERSUS PULL

How do we make change happen? In the 1970s Prime Minister Margaret Thatcher changed the deep structure of an entire nation within the space of five years. One of the most striking things about her approach was that she used many measures simultaneously. We call this 'the broad agenda' approach.

At one time the Scottish public was faced with no fewer than six proposals for statutory change in education alone. Now it is possible for the electorate to lobby their MPs to object to one proposed piece of legislation and have a small chance that they will succeed in modifying or even blocking it. It is scarcely possible to resist two, and certainly not possible, short of outright rebellion, to resist six changes. And this was only in the field of education. A lesson that we can learn from this for project management is that, if you want to force or push change into place, it is most effective to do this on all fronts at once. That way the people you are trying to change can scarcely resist!

Using force alone

Forcing change on to people is in fact the way most projects operate. The executive decides that change is necessary and decrees that it should happen. Senior management implement it with gritted teeth and a message of 'You've just got to do it. Get on with it or you're out!'. There are two disadvantages to this common approach:

1. It requires enormous effort and organization to set up and deliver the broad agenda. Margaret Thatcher was famous for her energy and taking little sleep. Her ministers were run ragged working to persuade their electorate and implement new legislation.
2. It is confrontational. Pushing people to change polarizes views and maximizes resistance.

Although some people enjoy fighting and winning, most people are uncomfortable about imposing their will on others too conspicuously. We tend to prefer a democratic approach based on fact and persuasion. In a project it is too easy for part or all of the project team to say, 'There – we've done our bit. We have delivered the IT or the new organization chart – now it's up to them to change.' It is very common for the intended changes to be quietly and successfully resisted, so that the company has both spent money on the project and failed to achieve the change expected to create the benefits and give the return on investment. This is akin to buying a new house successfully but failing to sell the old one, and consequently having to live partly in both and pay two mortgages.

Carrot and stick

A modification of the push approach to change is to use the 'carrot and stick'. What we can do here is to change people's perceptions so that they believe their current situation is, or is about to become, intolerable. For example, a company could say, 'If we don't make this change, the company is going to have to close all our UK factories and make all of you redundant. So you see, you really have no alternative but to accept these changes and comply with these new working conditions.' To give another example, local authorities might say to the fire brigades, 'Accept these new terms and conditions or go on strike. If you do strike, we are not going to give in and you will run out of money, public support and status. And by the way, don't blame us, mates – it's the government.'

Equally, the organization can make people perceive that the alternative future is irresistibly pleasurable – the carrot: 'The new terms and conditions will give those that remain higher consolidated basic pay. Overtime hours will disappear (without financial loss) so you will be able to spend more time with your families. Imagine the safer, brighter and better new assembly lines and working conditions. There will be many opportunities for you to learn new skills. With our new streamlined organization you can expect opportunities for promotion to really exciting and rewarding jobs.'

However, the iron fist of compulsion still underlies the change programme in this 'carrot and stick' approach. For the victim of change, there is really no option other than to comply.

ALTERNATIVES TO THE USE OF FORCE

Push, or to reveal its true nature, force, is a temptingly simple way of making change happen. But even setting aside any moral scruples people might have, it is economically inefficient. What are the alternatives?

Forcing change is in fact very expensive. In Chapter 2 we pointed out that large change programmes can cost as much as building a domed football stadium. So we must examine other ways in which large-scale change can be brought about, for less expense and with greater certainty of success. Here are two case examples.

Case 1

One of us was required to make fundamental changes within five months in the way in which an organization of 7000 personnel and 35 offices operated. However, there was to be no special budget for this work. Faced with this challenge, the first thought was: 'Well, if I use traditional project approaches the task is quite impossible. But if I perceive myself as having 7000 people to do the project with, it becomes very feasible.' This change was achieved by taking the radical steps of:

- designing the future state of the company in detail.
- describing practical, personal vignettes of how the future would be recognized when it happened
- communicating the future state very widely to everyone who was going to be affected – pretty well the whole 7000-strong community
- setting up a communication network to help people achieve the change
- implementing changes to the people's environment – accommodation, procedures and (eventually and not on the critical path), technology.

To be sure, an element of push and force was used. A relatively small, but significant, number of new posts were created and old posts removed. A small number of people were promoted into more senior posts and a slightly larger number of senior people moved sideways. The main task, however, was to communicate the future and then try to help people to adapt to it. This is the exact opposite of the traditional push project.

With this approach, people have the future described in personal terms to them until they reach the future state today in their minds. They are then helped to pull their current state towards the future state while the environment changes around them.

Case 2

Being the 'victim' of change of a 'pull' project is quite different from being in a 'push' project. To get an idea of this, consider this case. The organization introduced in Case 1 had earlier decided to change the working methods in one of its units. It commissioned a training video, made to full professional standards, to demonstrate the changes needed. This video showed actors performing the unit's work in the new ways, but set in the office environment familiar to the workers.

During one sequence in this video the actors were seen speaking to each other in Spanish (with no subtitles). 'That's right,' said the management. 'We shall need you to be able to speak with our clients in Spanish, because Spanish is the main language of more than half the business world.' The intended, and achieved, outcome was to get the people watching to ask 'When can I get my training in Spanish?'. This was in stark contrast to the reaction that would have been produced by the old 'push' project: 'I don't have time to go on any training. Let me get on with my day job.'

Chronesthesia

Cases 1 and 2 exploited the human brain's capacity for chronesthesia, which is the ability to imagine itself in a future state (explained more fully in the Glossary) and then adapt its perceptions to match.

When we watch a film or a video, especially one which uses storyline, music and visual cues to involve us emotionally, we actually change personality a little for an hour or so afterwards. It is as if we had lived for a short while in the world that we have seen in the film and gone through some emotionally charged experiences. It is some of this effect that we are capitalizing on to accelerate and simplify change when we use the pull, rather than push, option. However, 90 per cent of these changed perceptions are short-lived. In a change project it is necessary not only to prolong these changed perceptions, but also to make the change permanent. We do this is by telling the people who have to change that we shall be coming back later, to look for the changes that have been so vividly predicted and imagined.

INSPECTING AND MEASURING CHANGE

It is a principle of change management that 'whatsoever we measure we get'. In Isochron's pull approach to business change management we try, in the first instance, not to measure numerical targets so much as to inspect and recognize matters of fact. These are the recognition events and value flashpoints described in Chapter 3. By telling people about a small number of specific events that will signal the future state and then explaining to them that a particular manager will be coming to look at that event happening on a specific date in a specific place in the future we find that people are powerfully motivated to make the event happen.

When we measure anything, even a matter of fact, we have to establish the current state as a benchmark. Otherwise it can be difficult to demonstrate success. For example, many people involved in the £ tera-million preparations for Year 2000 found that senior management were cynical when the millennium passed without any IT hiccup. They questioned whether the invested effort and cost had been necessary. The benchmarks had not been adequately measured and communicated to them. They had not seen for themselves the clock in the BIOS on the PC motherboards flip to irrational values when wound forward to the stroke of midnight on 31 December 1999. They had not noticed the old and out-of-date PCs controlling the air-conditioning and security locks in their office blocks. They were not present when computer programmers found fatal bugs in their pension systems, and were even further removed from the same things happening in power stations, sewage processing plants and transport controls.

In managing business change, therefore, we have to take the recognition events and value flashpoints of the project and document their current state. Having done that, we must set up, at the *beginning* of the project, the arrangements to track the progress towards the occurrence of the recognition events and value flashpoints.

A MILITARY EXAMPLE

Cadets who enter the Royal Military Academy at Sandhurst will quickly discover that they must change if they are to do the things that the army expects of them: things that the rest of us have never done or will ever do in our lives. From the outset the training programme will present each cadet with powerful images of what the army expects him or her to become, using video, lectures and other effective induction experiences. One of the most significant images, signalling individual success in this programme, is the passing out parade. The cadets know from the outset that this will happen: it is inevitable and non-negotiable. Every Sandhurst cadet knows not only what this final parade will look and feel like but, more importantly, is also aware that it is going to happen to him or her. Each cadet knows exactly when this will happen and can imagine the pageant, with its music and air of occasion vividly (a strong example of chronesthesia).

The cadets know, in considerable detail, how they will be expected to dress for the parade. They know that they must march and counter-march to perfection, in step, in line and in sequence. This knowledge is greatly reinforced in every cadet's mind by the fact that the event will be inspected by the commanding officer, together with a representative of the royal family. From the point of entry to the course, there is no question whatever that the event will happen and, further, that it will happen exactly on the date and time ordained regardless of any difficulties that might intervene. *These images cannot fail to influence the performance of every cadet's work from Day 1 until the parade is done.*

This parade, as in any future army event or planned military action, is not, like a typical big IT project, going to slip a few months. The army could never allow that kind of lack of discipline. Thus, from the point of entry onwards, at the back of every cadet's mind and amongst many other images, is the intimate and detailed knowledge of what that important ceremony will be like and how its success will be inspected and measured.

If this chronesthesia, with its vivid images of a successful event under the eyes of critical inspection, can produce the desired results in the army, why not also in business? Isochron talks of 'an appointment with the future' and that's exactly what this process is. Once the appropriate image has been formed in the brain, it will transform the way in which the individual carries out his or her day-to-day job.

CONCLUSION

In this chapter we have stressed that the success of business change projects depends particularly on encouraging people to adapt to new situations and ideas. This process is best achieved by harnessing the minds of all those involved to perceive how they will exist and work in the new, changed environment. These imaginary images must include visions of how performance, measured in terms of recognition events and value flashpoints, will be inspected at precisely named future times and places.

The next, final chapter will extend this discussion, with a more detailed explanation of how we can understand and adapt human behaviour to enable the business to change.

REFERENCES AND FURTHER READING

CCTA (1997), *PRINCE 2: An Outline*, London: The Stationery Office.
Lee, B. (1979), *Introducing Systems Analysis and Design*, vols 1 and 2, Manchester: National Computing Centre Publications.

11 *Enabling the Business to Change*

This chapter concludes the discussion begun in the previous chapter on the role of people in business change and IT projects. It deals particularly with the conditions and factors that can influence the behaviour of people, our understanding of which is essential if we are to bring all the stakeholders on board to contribute willingly and effectively to our change programmes.

THE IMPACT OF CHANGE ON INDIVIDUALS

Because the ROI of the project and its business case depend not only on environmental and technology changes but also on people changing, the project team must have a deep understanding of the change from the perspective of those involved and affected – the stakeholders. If the stakeholders start to resist the changes that we need them to make it is both distressing for them and expensive for the project. Resistance to change will alter the whole business case – NPV, ROI and breakeven. In such circumstances we have sometimes heard senior managers say 'Well if they won't do it, fire them!' but, even leaving aside humanitarian issues, dismissing, replacing, inducting and training new staff is always a large cost that is not often fully allowed for in the business case.

From the project point of view we might consider applying change to whole groups of people or parts of an organization at a time. However, if we are to achieve success we must think of change from the point of view of those who will be affected by it, and especially of those who will be expected to contribute to it. What will the change, or indeed any change, mean to an individual? It is likely that you, the reader, will have experienced change in your job, perhaps many times. If so, the following scenario will be familiar to you.

- *Familiar processes on which you rely disappear.* For example, as part of the project to give up floor space and cut costs your company has hit on the convenient fashion of the secretary-less executive. From now on, you will have super facilities systems that let you manage your own travel bookings, diary and documents through your desktop or PC. But you will have to modify your working practices and schedule to find the time to learn the system and take on this new non-executive workload.

- *Skills and knowledge on which you have relied to underpin your status become redundant.* Suppose, for example, that you work in a public utility company and that you have the whole supply network of a neighbourhood in your memory. That knowledge and experience has made you a respected and essential senior supervisor on your patch. The change project is going to introduce new technology so that the supply network is mapped into a computer system. When that change is complete, even the most junior employee will have immediate access to information that is more detailed, up-to-date and accurate than your own memory. You will have lost your status as the unique source of this information in your organization.
- *Habits that have made you efficient and effective become unwanted.* For example, over ten years you have become reasonably proficient at using the old front office systems and you rely very heavily – indeed take for granted – the ingrained habits that let you make it 'sing and dance' for your work. Now you have discovered that the company is going to introduce a new and entirely unfamiliar system that you must learn and use for many months before you will be able to feel comfortable with it and achieve the same level of confidence and efficiency that you enjoyed with the old method. Perhaps you never will. And while you are learning the new habits, each day's workload will go on at the same level of pressure.
- *Your work location might change radically, increasing commuting time from home and adding to the length and stress of every working day.* The premises you have worked in for the last six years are to close as part of the project. But the place where you bought your family home was chosen specifically to allow you to walk to work. In future you will have to drive for over an hour at each end of the day, which must be paid for in terms of increased stress, reduced leisure time with your family and an additional £4000 a year in motoring costs. Your only alternatives would be to commute by rail (£3000 a year) or move house at considerable expense and at just the wrong time to move the children to different schools.

THE IMPACT OF CHANGE ON UNPREPARED ORGANIZATIONS

Anxiety, frustration and stress can also affect people collectively in parts of an organization that are committed to implementing change. An IT development group about to launch a system on which it has expended an enormous amount of energy, anxiety and millions of pounds might be heard to complain, 'We've done our bit and have developed a super system, but we can't get the business to implement it because they are refusing to allow time for training. The business isn't ready and it seems as if they never will be.'

Once a project team understands the reasons for such failures, it can foresee the need for important behaviour-related tasks and integrate these into its plan. Working backwards from the value flashpoints and recognition events which have been already communicated and illustrated to the stakeholders:

- Line managers must work to understand and act on the implications of the change as it will affect them and those working for them.
- Training has to be provided for each individual.
- Time must be allowed for individuals to make personal arrangements for change, both at work and in their personal lives.
- Time has to be planned for individuals to change their beliefs, attitudes and become accustomed to new habits.
- Backfill must be provided during the transition period to make time available for implementing the changes and training.
- On-the-floor support has to be arranged to prevent a drop in the performance, quality and productivity of day-to-day work until the changes become habitual: 'the way we do things round here now'.

In a large project these processes may take many months, maybe even more than a year. But this is a core part of every business change or IT project, not simply a fringe extra to that new building, relocation programme or new computer system. Failure to plan and manage these 'people change' issues will extend failure to the project itself. That is a common reason why projects do not produce the expected benefits, resulting in enormous costs and invalidating the capital and other resources invested in the project.

Such project failures extend beyond the projects in question and damage the corporate ability to undertake similar projects in the future. The workforce and its managers will become sceptical of anything new. The enthusiasm and cooperation necessary for successful change implementation will have evaporated. Failure to win people's hearts for change will even cause a decline in existing operational efficiency and increase fixed costs, all of which should have been predictable. Small wonder, then, that Isochron's business case studies frequently reveal the results of such poorly managed business change as the complete opposite of their investors' intentions.

HOW DO WE REACT TO CHANGE?

When a project leader announces change to the stakeholders, they will respond, as we all do, according to one of two classical models:

1. The person perceives that he or she can influence and control the change.
2. The person believes the change to be out of his or her control (as would happen, for example, in the case of learning that he or she has an incurable disease).

Suppose that you are a senior manager who has respect, authority and a powerful sponsor on the board. You hear about changes that the company has decided to make and learn about the project that will produce the change. You believe, with good reason, that you will be able to select and modify any of the changes which affect you personally. Perhaps you will be able to do the same for those reporting directly to you. You will probably travel through the response stages shown in Figure 11.1, as follows:

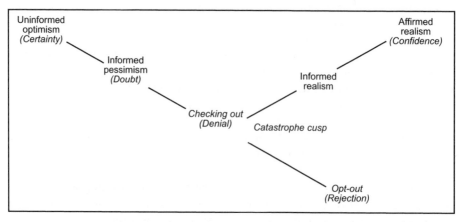

Figure 11.1   Human responses 1: to controllable change

1. *Uninformed optimism.* You know little about the change, so you fill in the missing information with optimistic assumptions. To your staff you present a confident and positive view. You may even be tempted into giving them assurances that you subsequently have to retract.
2. *Informed pessimism.* As you learn more, you find that your original optimism was misplaced. You begin to have doubts about the wisdom of some or all of the changes. You must, of course, continue to present a positive view to your staff, but you are developing a different (hidden) agenda behind the scene.
3. *Checking out.* You start to probe and ask challenging questions about the change. You can't believe that the proposals are true. If they appear to be irrational you can be sure that you don't have the whole agenda. You may start to deny that the changes will ever happen, at least not in the form you now know is proposed. You may be tempted to share this denial with your staff: 'There are some silly ideas in this change but they're misguided so I'm sure they won't happen. I won't let them happen anyway.'
4. *Informed realism (OR) or opt-out.* You realize at last that the changes will happen. You have to face up to it. It is possible that at this stage you will elect to rebel and refuse to make the changes. You may try to use your authority and your sponsor to block the project. This could end in dismissal or voluntary departure from the organization. Alternatively, you might learn enough of the hidden agenda to begin to accept the change. At this point you have to decide how

to change your position in relation to your staff. Can you share the whole agenda with them? If not, you may have to become a turncoat and accept loss of loyalty and criticism from your staff.

5. *Affirmed realism.* You convert to the new agenda and start to see the upside of the changes. At this stage you begin to direct your efforts towards helping to make the change happen. You guide your staff in the same direction. This is no light undertaking. Making change happen effectively often means completely wiping out the old visions and throwing out deeply rooted traditions. This can be as hard as eating your proverbial hat.

The process of rooting out bad traditions is very important. In an unpublished work, Professor Arvind Bhambry (then at the University of California) suggested that successful chief executive officers (CEOs) follow something like the following sequence when they join and fundamentally change a new organization:

*   *Phase 1.* They don't talk too early about vision. In the short term they build up personal credibility by focusing on short-term actions.
*   *Phase 2.* When they are ready, they act to wipe out – yes, wipe out - competing visions. This is where the deep-rooted traditions are thrown out. It's where the people who are at the informed realism stage either start to accept the change or opt out (possibly leading to voluntary departure or dismissal).
*   *Phase 3.* They align the executives and managers with the new vision.
*   *Phase 4.* They transfer energy to those who report directly to them. Critically, at this stage the CEO makes him- or herself a visible champion, sitting alongside the executives and senior managers as they transfer the new vision to their staff.
*   *Phase 5.* They make sure that the meaningful details are aligned with strategy. They walk the floor to check that the new operations match their strategy. This is exactly the same move as inspecting the recognition events and value flashpoints when the project reaches completion.

Now consider a situation where you are not a senior manager, have no special authority and certainly lack a powerful sponsor or protector. You hear about changes which the company has decided to make and about the project that will carry out the change. You believe, with good reason, that you will be unable to have any influence over the changes that affect you personally. In short, you have lost control of your future. You will probably go through the stages of response shown in Figure 11.2 and listed below.

1. *Stability.* You just carry on doing what you have always done. You hardly believe that the change is impending. You hear only what you want to hear.
2. *Immobilization.* After several repetitions you 'get the message'. Change that will affect you is going to happen, like it or not. Metaphorically, you freeze. This is akin to the moment of awful lucidity that happens when you are gravely injured. You know that you are about to feel a huge amount of pain, but right now it's painless and you can think very, very clearly.

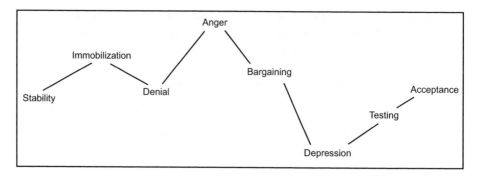

Figure 11.2 Human responses 2: to uncontrollable change

3. *Denial.* The news is so bad that you decide that it just can't be true. You are likely to tell other people that it is not true, that it can't be going to happen. 'It can't happen to me (or us) because...'. Both this and the immobilization stage perhaps contribute to the process of natural selection in nature. They give the threatened organism longer to think by postponing emotion that could cloud judgement about the best course of action. In this state severely injured people have remained conscious and have succeeded in struggling over considerable distances to seek help.

4. *Anger.* In a surge of emotion you attack the idea of the change. When you manage a project, do not underestimate the anger that impending change will create in some people. We have both witnessed scenes where such anger has erupted into physical violence. For example, some years ago, a senior manager in the civil service punched a union official in the face when he realized that the union was actually going to carry out a threat to walk out as part of its 'project' to change its members' working conditions.

5. *Bargaining.* When anger proves futile the emotion subsides and is replaced by an attempt to make a deal or plead your way out of the need to change: 'OK, I realize I've got to make time for that training, but couldn't we put it off until...?'; 'Fine, I know that the change is necessary, but my department could carry on if we just made this and this adjustment. We shouldn't throw the baby out with the bathwater, should we?'; 'Just give me a bit more time, that's all I ask.'

6. *Depression.* When anger and bargaining prove to be in vain you accept defeat and become depressed. In this state people may try to escape from the situation entirely. They will contemplate leaving this job, this place, *even this life*, and may actually do so.

7. *Testing.* If you cannot decide or simply don't get round to getting out, you are likely to start to explore what the change means. You test to see if there's any way in which you could make it acceptable. Maybe that new boss could be tolerated? Perhaps you could move house to that new location, after all? Perhaps the children could withstand a change of schools? Maybe it's worth hanging on just for the job. These reactions are possible whenever there's a chance, no

matter how slender, to turn the change to your personal advantage.

8. *Acceptance.* Inevitably, if you persevere you will start to accept the change. Sooner or later it will just become the new way of life. Perhaps it will turn out to be not as bad as you expected. Perhaps there are ways in which you will be able to make it tolerable, or even turn it to your own advantage.

The important thing to know, remember, plan for and manage, as a project manager, is that, no matter how trivial the change you think your project is going to impose on other people, you cannot know exactly what that change is going to mean to them. They will all go through one of the above change response cycles. Planning and managing those responses is as much a part of your project as the IT and construction work.

A manager said recently, half-jokingly, 'I should think our track record for benefit realization is about one half per cent of our expectations.' In fact, his organization had begun to take people issues more seriously, and its record was not that bad. But failure to manage the business change part of a project appropriately and not taking account of people's responses to the changes expected of them are fundamental causes of lost ROI.

MOTIVATION AND INCENTIVES

In his excellent and popular book, *Who Moved My Cheese?*, Dr Spencer Johnson offers 13 observations to the victims of change (projects) as follows:

1. Having cheese makes you happy.
2. The more important your cheese is to you, the more you want to hold on to it.
3. If you do not change, you can become extinct.
4. What would you do if you weren't afraid?
5. Smell the cheese often so you know when it is getting old.
6. Movement in a new direction helps you find new cheese.
7. When you move beyond your fear you feel free.
8. Imagining myself enjoying new cheese even before I find it leads me too it (recognition events; word pictures, videos of the future).
9. The quicker you let go of old cheese, the sooner you find new cheese.
10. It is safer to search in the maze than to remain in a cheeseless situation.
11. Old beliefs do not lead you to new cheese.
12. When you see that you can find and enjoy new cheese, you change course.
13. Move with the cheese, and enjoy it!

The point of this book (Johnson, 2000) is to help people to start to notice the need to change and to motivate themselves to make the change proactively.

We know that non-native organisms can multiply suddenly and dramatically, invading and destroying existing ecologies (Elton, 2000). Surprisingly, such invasions usually disappear again in due course with almost equal suddenness. An example of this is seen in the spread of some diseases, such as influenza. We can be reasonably certain that a particular strain of the 'flu virus will occasionally spread in a pandemic. If we had an idea of how to engineer such an invasion, but implanting desired beliefs and motivations rather than a virus, we could 'infect' a company with the change that our project demands. That would give us the key to causing the people side of business to change with some certainty and swiftness. Indeed, some organizations already talk of initiating change by 'a virus drop' and 'socializing ideas'.

In his book *The Tipping Point*, Malcolm Gladwell (2004) casts an interesting light on how we might create the climate for motivated change. He suggests that there are three rules of 'epidemics' in change, which are as follows:

1. *The law of the few*. This is connected with Pareto's 80:20 rule. It identifies a handful of exceptional people (Pareto's significant few) who connect with many other people and are regarded as 'cool' or admirable or role models and readily infect others with their behaviour. Thus when enough of these exceptional people in an organization accept and promote a change, they will abruptly start an epidemic of change across the whole company (creating a 'tipping point'). This confirms what we already know intuitively: that we should direct our initial communication and persuasion to the opinion-leaders. Once we have motivated a certain critical mass of these people, our desired change will propagate itself rapidly.

2. *Stickiness*. This is about making the message unforgettable. In large programmes it is not uncommon to find that a great deal of razzmatazz publicity is given to stakeholders at the outset. At that stage the message is vague. Unless someone has transformed the objectives into recognition events, the future vision will remain ill-defined and full of relative (and forgettable) terms such as 'improved efficiency', 'greater productivity' and 'a more driving organization'. Stakeholders find themselves in mass briefing sessions where many emotional words are broadcast at them, with the word 'excitement' occurring scores of times. However, there is a dearth of anything specific and personal that would give a stakeholder something to buy into. Enter the stability stage. The role models will sit there and let the messages go in one ear and out of the other. 'No need for any action on this,' they will say to themselves. It will become 'cool' to ignore the change.

    This suggests that we should make the change communications specific, personal and unforgettable. Perhaps that is why Isochron finds videos are so effective. Consider what was said above about what change can mean to individuals and Johnson's advice to the victims of change. It is clearly crucial to arrange that, in addition to being shown an unforgettable personal picture of the change, people have one-to-one, face-to-face management support as they go through the stages of response.

3. *Context.* Gladwell maintains that context is very powerful indeed. He suggests, for example, that one of the most significant reasons why New York City's crime rate dropped by more than 50 per cent in the period 1992–97 was that the environment was changed. Beginning with the subway, New York was cleaned of graffiti, broken windows and other environmental evidences of petty crime. Note that the first and effective action was not tackling the petty crime or zero tolerance. Instead, it was repairing the environmental damage faster than it could be committed so that the context looked different. Gladwell suggests that the problem is not so much criminals as criminal behaviour, and that criminal behaviour is triggered by contextual cues. There are many other examples. Note how, during the drought of summer 1976 in the UK, a single news item broadcast nationally saying that a hedgerow fire had been wilfully started by youths in one place led to a conflagration of such fires across the country.

This all suggests that, when changing the deep structure of a business, changing the physical environment is a good way of promoting behavioural change. This is convenient, because when we build buildings, change accommodation and implement new computer systems we are indeed changing the environment. Here, at last, there is a virtuous circle between what is often conventionally seen as the be-all and end-all of a project and the things that we should additionally be attending to. We have to manage the change that people are expected to undergo if we are to get our intended return on the investment in the project.

TOWARDS OR AWAY FROM?

When we set about constructing the specific future picture of a successful outcome to the project, we have to ask the sponsor and senior stakeholders how they will recognize success. What will happen and what will they see that will tell them their expectations have been met (recognition events)? However, we must ourselves recognize that about 40 per cent of people find it hard to consider a positive goal. These people are comfortable with identifying what they want to avoid (problems, failure, risks) but find it difficult to conceive something they want to attain, create or achieve. Shelle Rose Charvet (1997) identifies this proportion of the population as 'away-from-pattern' people.

A further 40 per cent of us are motivated by goals, objectives and futures. These are 'toward-pattern' people. They become impatient with away-from-pattern people, seeing them as hanging back and looking for obstacles rather than helping to move forward. Tim Smit, chief executive of the Eden Project, describes the immense task of creating and driving that project, which has created an environmental wonder of the world in Bodelva China Clay Quarry in Cornwall, UK (Smit, 2002). He seems to be an extreme toward-pattern person, as one would expect any such visionary to be, and it is striking how often in the project he experienced resistance from away-from-pattern people.

So, if 40 per cent of us are away-from-pattern and another 40 per cent are toward-pattern people, what of the remaining 20 per cent? Charvet's work suggests that this smaller group comprises people who exhibit a balance of away-from- and toward-pattern characteristics.

Of course, projects need people from both extremes. Without away-from-pattern people we would never identify projects that cure problems, and without toward-pattern people we would never embark on projects that create a better world. Without away-from-pattern people, toward-pattern people would have project disasters (they often do), failing to notice or manage risks and downsides. Without toward-pattern people projects would (and often do) sink into spirals of self-correction. Without one toward-pattern person and one away-from-pattern person this book would never have been written.

Isochron found that it is not necessary to have a special technique for discovering the recognition events in a project when toward-pattern people are asked to provide them (the toward-pattern people in this observation typically comprised a proportion of directors together with people in marketing and sales, and a proportion of middle managers and junior personnel). It takes these individuals about five minutes to learn what is required and then their desires and imaginations kick in with precise ideas about what they want to see happening when the project has achieved their expectations.

Conversely, Isochron finds that away-from-pattern people have difficulty with the whole concept of recognition events. Recognition events are out in the future, but the away-from-pattern person's mind is focused on how to avoid what is wrong now and what is about to go wrong in the near future. To overcome this difficulty, we have developed a technique that we call 'transfiguration'. First, we ask people (in a process that they usually enjoy) to compile a list of their complaints and problems. Next, we consider each item from the list and convert it into its exact opposite (antithesis). Each of these opposites represents a successful outcome. We place each of these successful outcomes at a specific future date and discuss the happy future (using people's capacity for chronesthesia) in an activity that is sometimes called 'future pacing'. Now we can derive the recognition events. Not infrequently, an away-from-pattern group starts the whole exercise in a depressed state. In those cases we can do some backcast planning, at least to start the process of tackling depression with action. Thus pessimism is converted to constructive optimism, allowing people to gain control of the future that they had previously feared.

The key point here is that we have to motivate and provide incentives for both away-from-pattern and toward-pattern people. If we try to deal with away-from-pattern people as if they were toward-pattern people we will make poor progress. Charvet mentions that television advertisements are prepared by marketing experts who are themselves largely toward-pattern people. Of their audience, 40 per cent are most likely to be away-from-pattern people, and they will be left unmoved by the prospect of owning that shiny new car or having that lovely bouncy hair. These away-from-pattern people are far more likely to be attracted by an advertisement that shows novel accident prevention design in a car door, or by the image of a lady suffering from dry, dead-looking tresses that are obviously in need of the proffered product.

When we consider how we are going to communicate with our Pareto few 'cool connectors', give messages that 'stick' and are unforgettable and change the environment, we need to understand that we are communicating with these two very different groups.

Away-from-pattern people typically hold the purse strings and allocate the budgets we need for projects. They have been given that budget authority precisely because they are away-from-pattern people. They represent safe pairs of hands. They will not risk spending the money unwisely. So, when they are also seen as 'cool' role models, we need to motivate them with talk of reducing risk, tackling difficult problems and proceeding with care, caution and proof. To show why an existing computer needs to be replaced, we will gather far more sympathy for our cause by demonstrating (with an analysis, images and forecast dates) the things that will inevitably go wrong if we do nothing and hang on to the old equipment. Singing the praises of the proposed new system will have little or no effect on these people.

Conversely, toward-pattern people are typically the champions of change. They are far more likely to regard a new project as an opportunity to enter a braver, newer world. But they are going to have to fight for their budgets and, indeed, they will rarely have been allowed to have control of one. When they are regarded as 'cool' role models we have little need to motivate them, but we must provide them with watertight business cases that will assure the away-from-pattern budget holders that the money will be safely invested.

CONCLUSION

The end-point to strive for in any business change or IT project is to achieve the outcomes (the ends, not the means) set out in the business case. The sponsor and stakeholders will be able to witness that these results have been achieved as they walk the floor and see the planned recognition events and value flashpoints happen. Reaching that successful condition obviously involves the implementation of environmental change (construction, accommodation, location and technology) but it is just as necessary to motivate people by implanting visions of their futures (chronesthesia) and thus help them to change what they do and where they will do it, how they will fit in the changed organization, how they behave and what they believe.

Getting people to change requires a deep understanding of what it is like for an individual to be confronted by change and how they are likely to deal with it. The project manager has to know how people are motivated, how to find the tipping point and create an epidemic. In Isochron's experience, this 'pull' approach is far more efficient and effective than a 'push' approach. People need to be offered support but be disciplined by the anticipation and reality of inspection. Those with authority and power need to know what they are going to look for from the outset and then to say 'I shall be coming to see the results'. And they must really go and look when they promised they would.

Isochron asserts that a project ends when all the recognition events and value flashpoints have happened and been witnessed. The value streams that flow from the value flashpoints will then be starting to deliver the return on the money and resources invested in the project. Those value streams must be sustained until the investment return period (18 months, three years, five years, ten years or whatever the financial authority has deemed right for the investment) is complete. Sustaining improvement involves disciplined personnel management, but it is also where IT comes into its own.

Nothing in this book requires current good practice and investment in previous methods to be discarded. However, we think that how you go about doing what the current good methods prescribe requires a radical rethink based on the techniques, arguments and evidences that we have set out. We believe that the way in which the world sets about doing business and IT change can be transformed and that this will accelerate projects, shortening their elapsed times by at least 30 per cent.

We shall be able to recognize this improved condition when we find people who begin their projects with visions of the successful outcomes. They will be able to identify the specific future events that will signal that their projects have met expectations. They will have learned to estimate benefits before costs, using probabilities and the Monte Carlo box. Investment committees will routinely screen and prioritize complete portfolios of projects, so that every project authorized is justified in business terms. Last but never least, we shall see that core parts of the project plan are assigned to the work of enabling people to change.

REFERENCES AND FURTHER READING

Charvet, S. R. (1997), *Words That Change Minds* , Dubuque: Kendall-Hunt.
Elton, C, S. (2000), *The Ecology of Invasions by Animals and Plants,* Chicago: University of Chicago Press.
Gladwell, M. (2004), *The Tipping Point,* London: Abacus.
Johnson, S. (2000), *Who Moved My Cheese?,* London: Vermilion (Ebury Press).
Smit, T. (2002), *Eden,* London: Corgi.

Glossary

This glossary assumes that readers are familiar with terms commonly used in project management and is primarily concerned with expressions that have particular significance to the Isochron methodology. For a general glossary of project management terms see PMI (2004).

abduction
Finding the factors that explain a situation; arguing backwards from an outcome or result. Compare with deduction and induction. *See also* **ascriptive episodes**; **backcasting**.

ascription
Attributing a cause to an outcome.

ascriptive episode
An episode where the events thought to have caused the outcome are associated with it as a matter of opinion, usually after the outcome has occurred. Projects are ascriptive episodes. *See also* **prescriptive episodes**; **descriptive episodes**.

backcasting
Using the desired end result of a project (the objectives or deliverables) as the principal basis and starting point for planning, so that planning is initially conducted by working backwards from project completion. The backcast sweep finds the minimum necessary path to the desired outcome. The process is very similar to techniques used in lean engineering to find the construction path or to explode the bill-of-materials from a finished prototype, except that it works backwards from *events* rather than from objects, IT or reports. *See also* **abduction**; **chronesthesia**.

bandwidth
Bandwidth is familiar to communications engineers as a measure of frequency spread but it is also used to express an organization's capacity in terms of people whose skills are key to its ability to perform several simultaneous projects. Fowler et al (1990) showed exactly how, and why, episodes (and therefore projects) are formally joined through shared

objects (resources). Thus a narrow bandwidth would put a constraint on the maximum possible size of the organization's portfolio of projects.

bandwidth analysis The process of focusing on the activities of people in the organization to determine how much of their time can realistically be set aside for project work. Isochron teaching includes the premise that project portfolios are constrained by the availability of people who are key to projects rather than by the sum of all resources identified in project plans.

breakeven point   The date when the benefit value returned first exceeds the directly associated investment.

Broadbent filter   The proposition that human conscious attention is single-stream (Priban and Broadbent, 2002). Broadbent also observed that speech and written communication are single-stream. Thus people are unable to attend to, listen to, speak or write more that one thing at a time. However, they can shift attention sufficiently fast to give them the sense that they are attending to more than one thing at once. Isochron observes that this limitation accounts for about one third of unnecessary sequential dependency in project plans.

chronesthesia   Defined by Tulving, (2002) as '[a] form of consciousness that allows individuals to think about the subjective time in which they live and that makes it possible for them to "mentally travel" in such time. There is no way in which the future, which does not yet exist, can influence anything that happens in the present – no way, except one: through a future that exists in one's conscious awareness of the world, the kind of awareness that chronesthesia makes possible. Chronesthesia is a trick that nature invented to circumvent its own most fundamental law – of the unidirectionality of time.' In Isochron methodology, chronesthesia is the mental capability to create and understand the desired end-state of a project, to create recognition events and value flashpoints, and to identify key milestones during backcasting.

concurrency   Planning and performing tasks concurrently, or at least allowing partial overlap, where traditionally those tasks would have been performed sequentially. Used to accelerate project delivery and in fast-tracking.

contract	A legally binding transaction between two or more parties where there is a clear exchange of services for consideration. Used in Isochron methodology to direct or steer projects by recognizing their contractual nature. The project contract within the PID identifies the deliverables and the investment (cost), so enabling a steering committee to use familiar disciplines of contract management to direct the project. Reduces the risk that the sponsor or steering committee will accidentally specify the *solution* instead of the *objectives*.
critical success factor (CSF)	A fact or influence essential to a result or outcome.
customer	The person, group or organization for which the project is being undertaken and to whom it is to be delivered. In internal management projects, where there is no external customer, the company (or a group within the company) is effectively the customer, and the project manager and his or her team act as supplier.
descriptive episode	An episode where the events thought to have caused the outcome are associated with it as if they were a matter of objective fact, usually after the outcome has occurred. Often confused with ascriptive episodes but confined to, and more or less synonymous with, prescriptive episodes. In post-implementation reviews, deterministic people readily confuse their opinion about causes with facts about causes.
discounted cash flow (DCF)	Cash flows adjusted using discount factors to find the present-day values of future costs and benefits. *See* **net present value**.
episode	A group of events that are part of a sequence leading to an outcome. An episode has a beginning, middle, end and an outcome. The outcome is the changed state of an entity or of a system of entities. Projects are episodes and inherit all the qualities of episodes, showing dynamic instability, entrainment, paradox and recursion.
episodic	Pertaining to episodes: having a duration. Contrast with facts. *See also* **semantic**.

episodic memory   *See* **Tulving's memory systems**.

event   Something that happens or takes place, changing the state of entities (objects). In a project, tasks bring about events, creating new outcomes. Events, because they contain sub-events, are also episodes. Hence projects are recursive. *See also* **key event; recognition event; milestone**.

event milestone   *See* **milestone**.

fast-tracking   A planning method that, using concurrency and other strategies, seeks to plan for the shortest possible project duration. *See also* **minimum necessary change**.

goal   Synonym of objective.

Isochron   Alternative spelling (US) of isochrone, which is a line on a map joining places where an event occurs simultaneously or where the journey time from another fixed point is the same. Used in the Isochron method to highlight concurrent events and focus attention on using characteristics of time.

key event   Another term for a milestone event, used particularly in activity-on-arrow critical path networks.

key performance
indicator (KPI)   A significant data measurement that indicates the level of progress towards a desired outcome.

milestone   Sometimes called a key event, milestone event or milestone activity, a milestone is a key stage in a project when a sub-goal of the project has been achieved. Milestones allow no gradation, but can only be perceived as achieved or not achieved (go or no-go).

minimum necessary
change   A term coined by Griggs (2003) to describe the path of least change, effort, cost, and time to reach the outcome. Not to be confused with the critical path in networks, because a critical path may be based on more than the minimum change and cost needed to meet the minimum time. Minimum necessary change underlies the effectiveness of Toyota's lean engineering of the 1970s and the step-change

in the effectiveness of shipbuilding by the Koreans in the 1980s. The Isochron approach uses backcast planning, abduction and concurrency.

Monte Carlo analysis
Performing very many iterations of a project cost estimate, project value estimate or project schedule in which the highest and lowest estimates of uncertain parameters are randomly substituted. The resulting curve or histogram shows the probability of any particular cost or time outcome within the overall possible range.

Monte Carlo box
A visually effective tabular presentation of Monte Carlo analysis results. It enables a simple way of using Monte Carlo analysis for practical application by project estimators.

net present value (NPV)
The present-day value of a sum of money spent or received at a future date. *See* discounted cash flow.

neuro-linguistic programming (NLP)
A branch of behavioural psychology that recognizes the way in which language programmes and reprogrammes the human nervous system. Developed by John Grinder, a linguist, and Richard Brandler, a mathematician and psychotherapist, it has become widely used in behavioural psychology. The Isochron method takes account of the fact that organizational behaviour and project performance are affected by words and stories current in the organization. Isochron applies NLP principles to organizations – for example, by requiring project sponsors and stakeholders to envisage and plan from the successful outcome of their expectations, so increasing the probability (or even ensuring) achievement. This contrasts with the tendency of 'what-if?' or worst-case planning to be self-fulfilling.

objective
Project objectives are usually expressed in relative terms, such as reduced staff costs, improved staff morale or increased sales. Sometimes there is an attempt to state objectives in absolute terms by adding numerical targets, such as 'Reduce hospital waiting times to 80 days' or 'Ensure that all deliveries are made in three days'. Isochron methods stress that numerical targets usually lead to unwanted behaviours, whereas behavioural targets usually

lead to required numerical outcomes.

objective transform A technique that links objectives to significant and visible events that key business stakeholders can recognize and expresses those events using plain English terminology that is easy to understand. *See also* **milestone**; **recognition event**; **value flashpoint**.

precedence diagram (PDM) The most commonly used form of activity-on-node (AON) critical path network diagram. A valuable feature is that the notation can clearly indicate overlapping tasks (partial concurrency).

prescriptive episode An episode comprising events that, for a given set of inputs, will always yield the same result. Examples are computer programs, machine operations and construction processes. Project sponsors, stakeholders and managers often mistake projects for prescriptive episodes; they think that, if they follow the steps prescribed by a methodology, experience or a project management software tool, the project will automatically achieve the required objectives. But a project is not a prescriptive episode. It is an ascriptive episode because of its interdependence with other episodes beyond the control of the project. Projects are therefore probabilistic, not deterministic processes: they respond better to abductive planning than to 'what-if?' planning.

programme A portfolio of some or all of the projects being conducted by a company or group of companies. Another (narrower) definition is a set of projects that contribute collectively to a business goal.

project There is hardly any need to define what we mean by a project, but that has not deterred many authorities from trying. Some definitions extend to hundreds of words yet still miss the essential points, which are that projects are ventures in which people or organizations set out to achieve prespecified results that are at risk because of the novelty and complexity of the total task. Unlike a large task, a project requires collaboration (and hence coordination) of resources to deliver the intended result. Consequently, it involves planning and the management of many people. *See also* **prescriptive episode**.

**project initiation
document (PID)**   Sometimes known as a project charter or project
                     specification, the PID is a formal document, similar to a
                     contract, which specifies the budget and level of resources
                     to be invested against a statement of the service or outcome
                     expected in return.

**project portfolio
management (PPM)**   Managing the appraisal, authorization and relative priorities
                     of all projects being undertaken by an organization so that
                     the project mix is the best for achieving the objectives of
                     the organization.

**project support
office (PSO)**   An office typically staffed with planners, progress chasers,
                     project finance managers, risk managers, change managers,
                     cost and benefit managers and quality managers, whose
                     function is to provide expert administrative support to one
                     or more project managers.

RAD   Rapid Application Development. A technique developed
                     by Scott Shultz in the US to accelerate the build of IT
                     applications. RAD requires that all the experts needed
                     for a project, including businesspeople with authority
                     and technical experts, are pretrained, fully equipped and
                     then effectively locked in a room to complete the project.
                     Infrastructure needed to launch the project (for example,
                     business readiness, databases, servers, and so on) is prepared
                     separately from the RAD.

RAG reporting   Red, amber, green (traffic light) reporting. *See* **traffic light
                     reporting**.

**real options
analysis (ROA)**   An analysis not of the benefits of the project objectives, but
                     of the benefits of the options that an organization might
                     gain by investing in the project. For example, by investing
                     in a project to change the IT infrastructure in a certain way
                     a company might gain the option of being able to outsource
                     the IT if it subsequently wanted to. A review of the value
                     flashpoints of a project against the value drivers of the
                     organization often reveals real options. A cash value can be
                     estimated for the value flashpoints of the real options

and included in the business case if this is in accord with Finance policy.

recognition event (RE)

A real-life happening that, when it occurs, tells a sponsor and other stakeholders that one particular expectation of the project has been met. REs do not have to be quantitative or numerical, but they must be events that can be recognized at a specified time and place. There is no limit to the number of recognition events for each project objective, but one is enough and most objectives have no more than three or four. *See also* **milestone**.

return on capital employed (ROCE)

The gross operating profit for an accounting period expressed as a percentage of the capital employed at the end of that accounting period.

return on investment (ROI)

The payback from the money and resources invested. *See also* **breakeven point; discounted cash flow; net present value; real options analysis**.

scripting

A term used by the social psychiatrist Eric Berne to describe the tendency that people have to repeat established behaviours. For example, a person who has been involved in a project that failed will be familiar with the situations that lead to failure. He or she becomes more comfortable with those situations than with (unfamiliar) successful behaviours. Isochron finds that organizations have their own scripts and that the scripts can be modified or changed by the same methods used by Berne and by NLP.

semantic

Pertaining to facts – *see also* **episodic**. Databases store semantic (not time-organized) data.

sensory gating

A term used in psychology and the study of the impact of drugs to describe the modification or removal of irrelevant sensory stimuli during pre-attentive phases of information processing, This gating reduces a person's conscious attention to just one thing at a time (*see* **Broadbent filter**). Exactly what is chosen to be irrelevant may be governed by many things including context, the person's experiences, beliefs and feelings and stimuli from language cues. This effect strongly influences the diversity of understandings of a single statement of objectives of a project and divergent views of planning, managing and participating in a project.

sponsor
The person who is responsible to a company or other organization for delivering the planned return on investment for a project or programme.

stakeholder
Any person, group or organization that can influence a project or will be affected to a greater or lesser degree by the project activities and their outcome. Stakeholders can be ranked as primary, secondary, tertiary and so on, according to the degree by which they can affect the project. In this book we are concerned mainly with the primary stakeholders, including the sponsors and managers of a project, the IT unit and the customer or end user.

steering committee
A committee that steers the project by providing authority, direction and resources. It manages the project 'contract' and has the power to stop the project and abort it if necessary. The committee is usually chaired by the project sponsor and consists of senior users of parts of the organization affected by the project (which includes the IT infrastructure), a quality assurer independent of the project, the project manager and a senior representative of finance.

traffic light reporting
A reporting method using the familiar red, amber, green phases of road traffic signals to highlight aspects of project progress or concern. *See also* **RAG reporting**.

Tulving's memory systems
Tulving (1985) identified and classified a number of memory systems and mental systems capacities, of which the following five are particularly relevant to the planning process:
1. Semantic memory – knowledge about the world. Example: 'I remember that Bill Smith has RUP skills'.
2. Episodic memory – remembering, with a time dimension, experiences. Example: 'I remember seeing that Bill had RUP skills when I read his CV last week, in the canteen during lunchtime and before I went to that meeting about staffing'.
3. Noetic consciousness – awareness of knowledge about

the world. Example: 'I am aware that I am thinking right now of the fact that Bill has RUP skills'.

4. Autonoetic consciousness – awareness of self in time. Example: 'I remember (myself) sitting in the canteen last week during lunchtime reading the pile of CVs and reading Bill's CV'.

5. Chronesthesia – awareness of subjective time. Example: 'I can recreate in my mind, as if it were now, the experience of sitting in the canteen last week during lunchtime, and how hot and stuffy it felt while I was reading Bill's CV and noticing that he had RUP skills'. Another example: 'I can imagine what it will be like to be in the training room on 23 September while Bill is using his RUP skills in scenario design'.

value drivers The things that increase revenue or reduce cost or increase asset value in the organization.

value flashpoint (VF) A recognition event (milestone) at which a particular project cash benefit starts to be realized. In the Isochron method, value flashpoints are used to map financial implications of the project to the business accounts, and to tie all project activity and investment to the points where the benefits start. An example of a recognition event which is also a value flashpoint is when a new product is first profitably sold to customers and the initial revenue is received. Conversely, a milestone signifying the end of a design phase is not a value flashpoint because it has no immediate cost benefit. Value flashpoints are the points at which the organization's finances are positively affected by the project. For example: 'The Quarterly Report for 30 June 2008 will show additional revenue from the specified new market' or 'The company accounts at end August 2009 will show the drop in servicing costs caused by replacing the old equipment'.

virtual company In order to carry out projects within exceptional time, cost and environmental constraints, some companies in the oil, gas and utility industries have created virtual companies for the duration of the project. A multi-supplier team is housed in a dedicated building with separate IT, files and administration. The team signs up to a special contract of behaviour and performance. The contract contains clauses to share out any savings made by accelerated performance in such a way as to encourage mutual support across the suppliers.

REFERENCES AND FURTHER READING

Fowler, A. K., Franks, D. J. and Currie, K. (1990), 'The Application of Parallelism in Commercial Dynamic Information Systems', *Proceedings of the International Working Conference on Dynamic Modelling of Information Systems*, TU Delft.

Griggs, Michael (2003), 'Minimum Necessary Change A Deliverable Strategy', at http://www.datawarehouse.com/?articleid=3198.

PMI (2004), *A Guide to the Project Management Body of Knowledge*, 3rd edn, Newtown Square, PA: Project Management Institute.

Priban, K.and Broadbent, D. (2002), 'Biology of Memory' in Baddeley, A., Aggleton, J. P. and Conway, M. A. (eds), *Episodic Memory: New Directions in Research*, Oxford: Oxford University Press.

Tulving, E. (1985), 'How Many Memory Systems Are There?', *American Psychologist*, 40, pp. 385–98.

Tulving, E. (2002), 'Chronesthesia: Conscious Awareness of Subjective Time', in D.T. Stuss and R. Knight (eds), *Principles of Frontal Lobe Function*, Oxford: Oxford University Press, pp 311–25.

Index

If you have found this book useful you may be interested in other titles from Gower

Advanced Project Management
4th Edition
A Structured Approach
F.R. Harrison and Dennis Lock
0 566 07822 8

The Relationship Manager:
The Next Generation of Project Management
Tony Davis and Richard Pharro
0 566 08463 5

Project Management
8th Edition
Dennis Lock
0 566 08578 X (hbk) 0 566 08551 8 (pbk)

Project Management A-Z
A Compendium of Project Management Techniques and How to Use Them
Alan Wren
0 566 08557 7 (A4 hbk) 0 566 08556 9 (A4 Loose leaf)

The Project Manager's Guide to Handling Risk
Alan Webb
0 566 08571 2

Using Earned Value
A Project Manager's Guide
Alan Webb
0 566 08533 X

GOWER

Law for Project Managers
David Wright
0 566 08601 8

The Bid Manager's Handbook
David Nickson
0 566 08512 7

Gower Handbook of Project Management
3rd Edition
edited by J. Rodney Turner and Stephen J. Simister
0 566 08138 5 (hbk) 0 566 08397 3 (CD-ROM)

Benefit Realisation Management:
A Practical Guide to Achieving Benefits Through Change
Gerald Bradley
0 566 08687 5

Failsafe IS Project Delivery
Andrew Holmes
0 566 08255 1

50 Checklists for Project and Programme Management
Rudy Kor and Gert Wijnen of Twynstra Management Consultants
0 566 08278 0

For further information on these and all our titles
visit our website – www.gowerpub.com
All online orders receive a discount

GOWER